L
  O
    V
      E

H
  O
    P
      E

S
  T
    R
      E
        N
          G
            T
              H

The ride and this book are dedicated with love to my Phoenix

Dave Spragg

'Fight back with all that you are'

Lydia Franklin

ISBN: 978-1-326-77335-9

PublishNation

www.publishnation.co.uk

Foreword

I've been fortunate to work alongside Lydia for many years and I am so grateful for all her enthusiasm and support in assisting me with the running of the Love Hope Strength Foundation UK.

Lydia is an incredible person who gives 100% to all that she tackles in life. I continue to be amazed and heartened by witnessing her adventures... Cycling Route 66, Cycling across New Zealand and now the Tour Divide! I am very proud to call Lydia my friend and I look forward to a million more adventures on behalf of Love Hope Strength with Lydia by my side.

Jules Peters

The Phoenix: In ancient mythology The Phoenix is a bird that dies and then is re-born, rising out of the ashes of it's past life. It appears in a myriad of cultures and represents renewal, protection, transformation, strength and balance in life, amongst other things. For me it is a symbol of the spirit of a human being and it's capability to overcome obstacles and difficulties. My Phoenix watches over me and keeps me safe and inspires me to keep going when it feels like all is lost. It gives me strength when I have lost all mine.

New Zealand: Also known as Aotearoa – Land of the long white cloud, New Zealand is made up of two land masses, the North and South Islands located in the southwestern Pacific Ocean. Sparsely populated with only around 4.5 million people, it is known for it's spectacular landscapes, vast mountain ranges (uh oh!) steaming volcanoes and stunning coastline. With a general mild and temperate climate, it can vary greatly between North and South, with the North Island experiencing sub-tropical temperatures, while the South is much cooler. It's a green country so there can be plenty of rainfall, especially on the West Coast of the South Island (Uh oh again!) Around 1500 miles in length, people drive on the left (yay!) and English is the main spoken language (Yay again!) My route is shown on the map below.

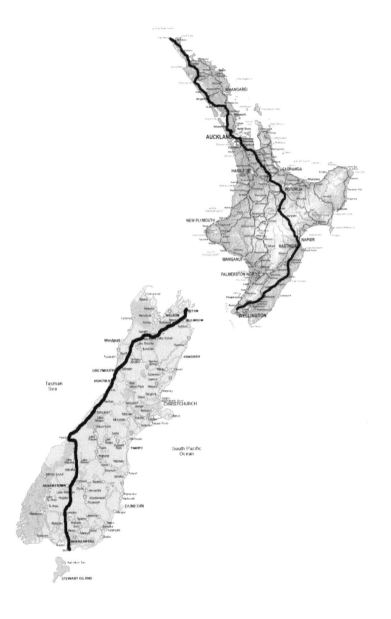

Who am I.... ?

Well damn that is a good question!! I'm not always sure myself. If asked my friends... and I generally don't because I worry about the replies I would get ... I imagine the majority would describe me as a CraZy stubborn fool, which I consider considerably better than boring. Following a mid-life crisis at 30, I have embarked on a life where there is an adventure in the planning or doing stage at all times, filled with music and friends and a charity called Love Hope Strength. In my other parallel life, I masquerade as a serious professional (well maybe not so serious), working as an Advanced Neonatal Nurse Practitioner in the Royal Berkshire Hospital in Reading, one floor up from where I was born! I love my job... it provides a challenge, laughter and the occasional adrenaline rush. Supported by some fantastic dedicated colleagues and a couple of wonderful (and sometimes concerned) work mothers who help keep my feet on the ground. I have transformed the path of my life several times, joining the Royal Navy out of school, leaving to fall into Nursing and become a step-mother to two beautifully wonderful children (now adults) and then as my marriage broke down, becoming involved with The Alarm and Love Hope Strength Foundation and filling my 'spare time' swabbing people for the bone marrow donor list at gigs and festivals and organising the volunteers for the charity, reaffirming my faith in the 'human being' and receiving inspiration to make the most of life. I am proof that re-invention can happen and that you don't have to settle for the person you have become or the life you find yourself in. Like the Phoenix I have risen from the ashes of my life more than once and that capability resides in all of us.

This is not the first time I have embarked on such Craziness..
Nearly three years ago I set off on 'a journey of a lifetime' with the aim to cycle Route 66 in 24 days. 100 miles a day, horrible headwinds, disastrous downpours and dastardly dogs made it a difficult challenge but set a course where I would no longer be happy with a jaunt up the road on my bike. That story has been told in my

book 'Putting the Metal to the Pedal' which is also available on Amazon, the proceeds from which are donated to Love Hope Strength Foundation. That journey taught me many things about myself and despite being a totally different experience from New Zealand, the lessons I learnt there stood me in good stead on this massive undertaking.

I am complicated, so much so that I confuse myself on a regular basis.

I love to push myself and challenge my limits of mind and body.

I love the peace and quiet of being on the road with only myself to rely on.

I love the outdoors and hate cities.

My head is filled with dreams of the things I want to try and the places I want to experience.

I have no religion and believe that this life is all you get, which drives me forward relentlessly.

Oh… and I HATE being chased by dogs!

So that's me in a snapshot… the detail is found in the story of this journey.

The Gates of Hell...

...... The main problem was that I didn't know what I was really facing... it could be another Rimutaka ... it could be worse... it could be better... the mind conjured up scenarios of me still climbing the pass at 4 or 5pm... then what?? Being wet and very cold made it clearly worse and then I passed through the Gate of Haast (gate of hell more like) which signified the start of the proper climbing. 15-20% in places I reckon... with an escape hill on the opposite side of the road... (that tells you how bad it was!).. and gears that were slipping drove me to the very edge of breaking point. I was absolutely certain I wasn't going to be able to finish today... ..

You may not believe how close I was to stopping.. or how desperately I wanted to sit down and close my eyes... be warm and dry at home... or how the tears ran down my face in frustration at myself for being weak...

Dream ...

I didn't expect it to be easy. In fact that was the whole point of this journey. Yet another venture into the world of pain and suffering, to exorcise whatever demons I harbour that make me want to push myself to my limit and then beyond. Perhaps by the end of this book, you will have a greater understanding... maybe I will... maybe it will remain unexplained...

The seeds of this journey were sown two years ago, out on the road called Route 66, when having too much time to think, coupled with what was probably an easier day with beautiful scenery, made me think that another 'journey of a lifetime' was a great idea. Once back on my feet at home, the pain forgotten, the noise of the headwind howling past my ears consigned to memory, the planning began for another epic challenge. Anyone who read my book 'Putting the metal to the pedal. Cycling route 66 with Love Hope and Strength' may feel that the seeds of Go With The CraZy were sown long before that.

Aside from my upbringing, where I was encouraged to follow my dreams and persevere with tasks I set myself, (sometimes landing on deaf ears because of my streak of stubbornness perhaps!), my more recent association with Love Hope Strength Foundation, Mike Peters and his wife Jules, have demonstrated to me over and over again how you must grab hold of life and shake the hell out of it. Since being involved with The Alarm and Love Hope Strength I have had many opportunities to Dream aloud - playing my guitar in Abbey Road studios and being part of a Guinness Book of Records song, flying to Vail to take part in Vail Rocks, drinking in the Houses of Parliament Stranger's bar, playing my guitar onstage with Mike , eating curry with Captain Sensible and Slim Jim - all moments in time that would haven't occurred were it not for Love Hope Strength. Then there were the jaunts on a bike - first South to North Wales, then from Snowdon Rocks to Nevis Rocks, then Route 66... each ride getting bigger, longer and harder. Each ride presenting their own challenges, each ride teaching me more about the tired, weak, hungry, cold version of me. They were also my chance to pay it forward - do some good in return for all those opportunities that I have been lucky enough to be able to grab hold of.

Why exactly I feel the need to go and cycle CraZy distances in as short amount of time as possible, I'm not quite sure... nor am I asking you for an opinion in this subject as I'm worried about the answers I would get. The fact remains that something in my psyche craves the solitude and mental and physical test that these challenges provide. A need to find out about myself when I'm at my lowest ebb and a need to have only myself to rely on, prevails over all other voices shouting at me (mine and others) to just go and sit on a beach for a week - something which I would find impossible to countenance.

A large part of the prompt for a new dream is the craving of simplicity ... Let me explain... simply put... life on the road is devoid of complication, choices are black and white, grey areas fade into obscurity and life tunnels into three things.. shelter at night... eating to fuel the body and turning the pedals.... thats it! Life is reduced to the very basics. Think Maslow's hierarchy from bottom to top. Home life for me is a whirlwind of work, gigs, people, clutter. All very good and exciting but clouding to the mind. Occasionally in all this, the whirlwind stops for a second to reveal a moment of peace within - the eye of the storm - and it takes a practiced eye to catch and appreciate these moments. For example, seeing babies born for me is an everyday occurrence - just part of my work - but every now and again, I stop and appreciate the fact that I am there at the moment that a baby takes it's first breath ... a simple thing. And then the eye of the storm passes and the whirlwind begins again. Out on the road, basic things are uncertain...there is no guarantee of a hot meal at the end of a long hard day... warmth is not a given and usually a rarity... occasionally even life is under threat (whether real or imagined, it makes no difference). Therefore every little thing that can be, becomes a source of enjoyment, contentment, peace, happiness and things that are taken for granted are cherished in a way that isn't always possible in a whirlwind. And that is addictive.

Being a small entity in the vastness of nature also reminds you of the finite nature of the bigger journey of life .

It is these things that prompt the dreams. It is these things that propel me back to the road.

I have also discovered that the best way to 'feel' a country is to experience every (often painful) inch of it. Travelling by bike allows me to suck up the atmosphere of a country and sear it into my soul in a way that driving in a nice warm comfortable car, and hopping out at the tourist attractions doesn't provide. I may miss some of the 'must see' places but in turn I will have really 'seen' the country and the people.

If one should read a certain tabloid newspaper, you could be forgiven for believing that the world consists of only murder, rape, suicide, bombings and evil. You could be forgiven for never setting foot outside your front door, let alone out into the wider world, where if you weren't hijacked on the way, or blown up once there, you would almost certainly be killed by a rampaging axe murderer. But if you fight the fear and take a few tentative steps outside, you would find that not only are people not axe murderers but on the contrary are people who want to help you, are interested in your story and have one of their own to tell and many of whom will go well out of their way to ensure that you are safe and well. At least that is what I have encountered in well over 4000 miles of cycling these crazy challenges. And that is another thing I carry with me after a ride… a restored and reaffirmed faith in the human race.

New Zealand presented a different challenge. For someone who isn't exactly a natural mountain climber (think Mark Cavendish rather than Nairo Quintana), New Zealand was a CHALLENGE!

Less mileage than Route 66 by about 1000 miles - in terms of feet climbed it was like Everest next to Ben Nevis - almost literally. Why did I pick New Zealand then - if I am not a mountain climber - surely the Netherlands would have been a better option?? No it wasn't because Lord of the Rings was filmed there! Precisely because it would make it tough and in my mind - people wouldn't sponsor me if it wasn't considerably tougher than Route 66. I also have a love of mountains and lakes and rivers and New Zealand promised these in abundance, along with the requisite solitude from mankind. More importantly - I have never been and it seemed like a good excuse! (A variation on Mallory's 'because it's there'!)

So the dream was there and in order to turn it into a reality, the next step was to....

Plan....

Whilst many of you may think that I get stupid ideas and then just go out and do them, you don't realise that you have missed out the most vital and often most enjoyable part - the planning! My Dream...Plan ...Do philosophy hinges on the plan part. New Zealand took 2 years to plan - from conception to getting on the plane - with every little detail examined under a microscope.

First the time frame - which constrains the possibilities or more accurately, sets the level of suffering intended. In my case 4 weeks was what I had to get over there, get it done and get back. Lucky in my choice of job and more importantly understanding colleagues (work mothers) meant that I could take this time off with the knowledge that I would have to work my arse off when I got back. The time frame then informs the route by dictating what is possible. Here for the most part I was guessing as to what mileage would be doable within a day given the mountains that stood between me at the northern tip and me at the southern tip. Part of this guesswork came from my previous experience in America, where I completed an average of 100 miles per day of cycling, with less climbing. I reasoned therefore that an 70-80 mile average may not be unreasonable and worked on that totally 'scientific' calculation. My mind does generally tell me that once I have said that that is the plan - I will find a way to stick to it, so once I had settled on that it was time to plan the route in greater detail.

Things that inform the route planning other than mileage are places to stop and eat, sleep, find provisions. The bike packing revolution had been somewhat belatedly introduced to me and I pursued this wholeheartedly. Bike packing is about travelling light, very light. Although my kit in America had barely weighed 20Kg, there were many items that I had taken which I had no use of or could have done without. A rack and pannier set up has been outmoded by bike packing bags - one under the seat post, one in the frame and optionally a bar bag. With less space to put kit, reason dictates that you take less kit! And so it was. Months of research led me to a tarp and bivvy bag set up as an optional just in case. Much lighter than a tent and generally quicker to set up and pack away - it was ideal for emergency shelter or if I got stuck in a place between civilisation. Whilst I did intend to motel it mostly- my hope was to spend a few nights outside stargazing.

So if motel was the general choice of nighttime accommodation - then I would have to plan each day to end in a town where one was available. this sounds simpler than it is, when terrain and mileage has to be taken into account. Some days looked like 100 miles of mostly climbing, whilst a few were 60 miles of easier terrain, in order to avoid an 120 mile epic due to lack of places to stop between the 60 and the 120 mile marker.

The other thing I took into account was my tourist day off! I was determined to walk on Franz Joseph glacier. This plan however necessitated me taking the mildly 'hillier' side of the south island - but so be it. Pain for gain - Right? The route was then mapped out mile by mile on Map my Ride, then Ride With GPS, giving me detailed climb data of the route I intended to follow. (I even 'Google First person'd' some of the days I was to ride, going on to google maps - zooming in as far as possible and then following the route). I have to say that I didn't look too closely in case I scared myself, but I did notice that there were a few 'epic' days which had over 80 miles and 6000-8000 feet of climbing. I then ignored that small fact and concentrated on picking my gear.

Gear, a small word for something that took up so much of my time. Care has to be taken in picking the right kit. I had decided early on that I would be taking a road bike. Lighter and faster than a touring bike, it should be comfortably be able to carry what little kit I was taking. Once I had my lovely sleek racing machine (a Giant defy 3), I set about making plans to make it ugly with various attachments and add ons. It then got nicked from my home, causing a huge amount of stress and annoyance with a little local publicity for the bike ride (every crap thing has a silver lining right?) - so I upgraded to a Giant Defy 1 and proceeded to do the same to my new bike. More upsettingly, the bike I rode Route 66 on, which had carried me safely for all those miles was also stolen. Unreplaceable in terms of the memories it held - that was far more devastating and unbalancing to the soul then my new bike. To my new Giant Defy, Aero bars (not the kind you eat) were bolted on and the frame was hidden beneath two top tube bags and a frame bag. Wobbling precariously, at least until I had worked out how to attach it properly, was my seat pack, where the bulk of my kit would reside. All the bags were purchased from Apidura on the reasoning that this was the kit that Trans-Am and RAAM (Trans-America and Race Across America) racers used, therefore it must be good. One eye was on future plans and an opportunity to test this kit for greater plans was also in the back of my mind.

My sleeping system, as previously mentioned was a tarpaulin and bivvy bag. A lightweight sleeping bag, a sleeping pad and a sleeping bag liner completed the 'look' and I was satisfied that I would be dry, relatively comfortable and hopefully reasonably warm. the sleeping bag liner had been added due to worries about being caught out up high. I have previously camped in March in the Peak District with a few feet of elevation and had numb feet for the best part of half a day. Losing toes to frostbite didn't appeal, hence the extra layer just in case!

Clothes was easy - as few as possible. I wasn't worried about having to wear the same clothes over and over again as I only had to put up with myself. 2 sets of cycling kit and one set of off the bike clothes sufficed. Not much for 4 weeks but even then I was debating whether i was taking too much. Wet weather gear was more important and a lightweight rain jacket and showerproof gillet were added along with arm and leg warmers for those chilly descents. Emphasis was placed on packability and weight. The smaller and lighter the better. Tools were likewise easy as my limited mechanical skills dictated how few tools i need. I can fix a few things on my bike - punctures, broken chain and cleats for example but many things are beyond me, especially in the middle of nowhere so that narrowed down that tools I needed. A bike tool, chain tool, pedal wrench and spoke key were all I took. spare chain links and spare spokes along with 4 inner tubes were the extent of my replacement kit.

Most of my research was dedicated to electrical kit and how to charge it up as well as staying connected to the outside world as much as possible for begging purposes. I discovered out on Route 66 that by far the most important thing to help keep me going was this connection to family and friends and therefore electrical kit took up far more space than it should have. I had a solar charger, a spare phone battery, a power bank and all the cables that that entailed. Rechargeable light, GPS unit, 2 phones (one NZ one) a camera, an action cam and a tablet completed the electrical roster. The GPS unit was technically unnecessary as the route was pretty simple and offline maps would have sufficed but again with one eye on future plans, this was my opportunity to test it out! Loading up the maps was a challenge and a testing run was disappointing but perseverance was the key and by the time I left for NZ I had a track to follow. The bonus of the GPS Garmin Etrex 30X was that it ran on AA batteries and had no need to be recharged.

Gradually more and more bits got added to my kit list and soon my bedroom resembled an expedition warehouse! All spare space was given over to this latest exploit.

Flight booking was the next thing and I hit a slight hitch - I had originally planned to leave a week in between The Gathering (a weekend long music gathering of The Alarm) as I knew the weekend would be only punctuated with sleep but necessity dictated that I be back at work for the week that all the Junior doctors swopped over. So the only way to do it was to leave the day after The Gathering finished. Suck it up basically. Go to N Wales - have little sleep the entire weekend, drive home, put my bike in a box and go to the airport. that's the way it was, that's the way it had to be. Again my brain digested and then accepted it and the trip was a go!

Training… a dirty word in my book. there is nothing I hate more than 'having' to go out on my bike and complete a requisite number of miles. Don't get me wrong - I love going out on my bike but attach the word 'training' to it and suddenly it seems like the worst thing in the world. Add to that the fact that because i was leaving in February, most of the training would have to be done on dark, wet cold winter days. I'm not a fair weather cyclist by any means but I do prefer riding on sunny warm days and i found it hard to force myself out. Therefore very little training got done, certainly less than the minimum 40 miles twice a week standard that I had set myself pre Route 66. I reasoned that I had good baseline fitness, that you couldn't train properly for 80 miles day after day, that the first week was going to hurt whatever training I did.

The one important thing that I did was take my bike out for a 'fully loaded' training run, to bed down all kit and find anything that was severely wrong with my set up. It didn't go so well....

.....Lessons Learnt - Part one

It all started with too much time driving in the car back from snowy Scotland.... too much time to think and plan.

I rang my mum. Tomorrow I'm going to cycle a long way with all my kit and Can I possibly set up camp in your garden tomorrow... oh and tea would be great too. Now my parents being my parents and having set me on the path of who I am today... did not question the sense behind camping in January with kit meant for a summer in New Zealand and temperatures to match... instead the question I got was.. and what time will you be here for dinner??

So that was that. In fact... details of freezing temps aside... it was actually a sensible plan... to try to find out any problems with the kit in an area I knew and if necessary could be easily rescued from... should all go completely pear shaped. The camping thing was basically... if I can survive January in the UK then NZ will be fine... so went the theory.

So when I arrived home my plan was to pack ready to just leave in the morning...

Plan ruined by food and that tired sleepy feeling... probably caused by two excellent days in the snow covered hills but herein lies... LESSON Number 1 (of many today). .. Always get stuff ready the night before... no matter how tired you are... because otherwise you find yourself waking at 5am.. scrambling around to get stuff done... only to leave later than planned... with things not done properly... but more of that later.

So I set off at 08:45 (planned for 8)

As you can see I was smiling... it wasn't raining and although chilly... wasn't ridiculously cold.

I had uploaded a route to my GPS to check it out and see how it worked... not great. Clearly I haven't read the manual but it wasn't prompting me to turn at all. I can see the track I needed to follow on the map but no prompts to turn.. sound or visual. If anyone knows what i did wrong... Matt Dixon.. Mark Davies... any other cycling nuts out there... please message me!! So I spent the first 6 miles... stopping and starting... pressing buttons... and generally trying to make it work. Then I gave up and just kept checking the track on the map and following it... and that was fine. And then I started to enjoy the ride.... LESSON Number 2.. don't rely on technology!

It didn't stop me seeing the deer that ran across my path though ... and that made me smile.

Shortly after the photo above I had turned off the main road onto a smaller paved track... cycling merrily along... when I encountered a puddle. No I wasn't being overly precious about my lovely new road bike... this puddle was the width of the road and looked deep. Sod it! I had overshoes right. Ankle deep water turned into calf deep water and I struggled to keep forward momentum whilst all the time expecting to just disappear up to my neck in muddy water. It looked a bit like this...

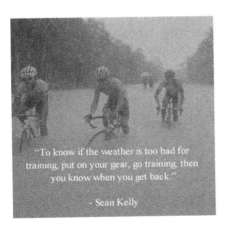

"To know if the weather is too bad for training, put on your gear, go training, then you know when you get back."

- Sean Kelly

And I'm not exaggerating this time...

Fortunately neither did I fall off or plunge into an underwater chasm and emerged from the 'puddle' a bit wet .. but chuckling out loud! LESSON Number 3 - If it looks deep... it probably is!

So on I went... and here is the part you might slap me for... no breakfast... I know I know... anyway I was starting to feel a bit crap so stopped and ate a cereal bar and ingested a gel to ward off the inevitable... coming at me like a train... cycling bonk. No (you dirty minded lot) I'm not being rude. It's the cycling terminology for when you hit the wall and have nothing... none... zip.. energy left. Wasn't quite there yet... so on I continued. LESSON Number 4 - Always... Always have breakfast where possible!

It was this point that my route planning was found to be very 'Lid like'. Not content (David and Nic substitute road for path here) with the easy tarmac I headed off (following the GPS track) the road and instead followed the 'road' .. which in this case started off as a gravel track and quickly became a muddy... rutted... stone filled... tree branch dotted... road. I hadn't been planning a spot of cycle cross but this was a good impression of it for sure. I kept my fingers and toes firmly crossed as I bounced in and out of water filled holes.. across sharp stones... over roots and other assorted obstacles. 2 miles later... I emerged victorious with wheels/tyres/frame and chain intact onto David and Nic's definition of a road (if their path definition is anything to go by)

So no worries about my tyres on 'bad roads' then. I did shed a tear over the state of my once pristine bike

I reached the northernmost point of my planned ride and halfway and to be fair... despite being slightly tired the cyclocross had re-energised me a bit and I stuffed another cereal bar ready for the second half. It was all downhill from here... right???

Part 2 coming shortly....

15

Lessons Learnt - Part 2

So where was I.... oh yeah... heading like the proverbial steam train towards bonking big style...

Funnily enough the two cereal bars and gel didn't halt the decline and in short order I found myself at the lowest ebb possible... worse than the headwinds in Arizona and the hills in Missouri combined. (Search for 'Putting the metal to the Pedal' on Amazon to read my book about my American experience)

And so when I reached this point I had a choice... continue on the planned route... or hightail it to my 'campsite' for the night.

I battled with my headspace for a good five minutes before deciding to continue onwards ... at least for a bit. Food was now a necessity in order to put fuel into my now useless legs. So I made a slight detour to a co-op... made the cashier laugh when I explained I wouldn't need a bag because I was just going to eat it on the spot... and pulled over to a nearby bench to eat my lunch....

Lunch was interrupted by the two town crazies... one of whom accused me of flashing... explained by my rear bike like... the other repeatedly asking me where I was from.

So when the rain started gently falling.. it provided a handy excuse to jump on my bike and making my speedy escape. It was actually more like clamber ungainly onto my bike and escape slower than the disabled scooter crazy number 2 was riding. Oh well.

It was around this time I looked up to see a Chinook helicopter hovering overhead and my first thought was 'yay its come to rescue me' ... bit it wasn't to be and my tired legs were forced ever onwards.

The rain now pelting down was at least washing the mud off my bike somewhat and in my head made it slightly lighter.. but the legs were still screaming at me on the ever present uphill. I was in familiar territory.. which provided a good excuse when I decided to switch my front light on to discover it had no charge (back to LESSON Number 1) ... Lesson number ?5... always charge stuff up the night before. I therefore needed to be back before it got dark...

having no front light (shhhh don't mention the head torch) and decided it would be wise to cut across a portion of the route to shorten it a little.

So across I went... up and down dale.. just turning the pedals ... struggling up the hills... and resting on the aero bars (not for the aero effect... chocolate or otherwise) to give my poor cramping hands a bit of a break.

At one point I saw a big bird (red kite) rising majestically up from the middle of the road just in front of me... to my knackered brain... it was as if my phoenix had risen up to show me the way... and it did make the next ten minutes or so feel betterer.

I counted down the villages as they passed... marking in my head the way home. Nettlebed... Peppard, Sonning Common and finally Caversham... WAYHEY!
I knocked/keeled over onto my parents door and collapsed in a heap inside...
I had a coffee in hand and was sitting by a fire in short order... reasoning that both MAY be found at a campsite. The restaurant of mum and dad was open for business and a huge amount of calories consumed!

Ride stats then: 60.79 miles... average speed 12.1 (bit slow) ... Max speed 36.1mph (how the hell..????) And total moving time of 5:00 hours. So not too bad... with all my kit.

And what of my plan to camp outside you may ask.. bet you think Ive chickened out right??

Tarp was set up in five mins flat... air bed inflated and sleeping bag stuffed into bivvy bag on top of air mat. Its pretty cool. Maybe wont completely protect me but if I survive this... NZ wont be a problem.
Essentially... if I think I may be developing a problem overnight that could jeopardise my getting on that plane in a couple weeks...

then I will head inside... but I'm talking about frostbite... not lack of sleep or being merely cold. That said ...leaving the fire will be hard so I may be 'in bed' later than usual ..lol.

So check out my fb page tomorrow... see if I survived...

And for those that were waiting for the pain and suffering to begin before sponsoring me... www.justgiving.com/GoWithTheCrazy is the link! (*For anyone reading this now the journey has finished - a donation can be made to Love Hope Strength via Justgiving at* https://www.justgiving.com/lhsf *)*

My kit will stay inside in the warm and dry tonight minus all the clothes I have in my kit which I will be wearing.... so as you snuggle up in your nice warm bed... have a thought for me before you drift off.😁

LHS

I did survive - well until about 2 a.m when I woke up so cold that I reasoned that the bigger picture of getting to New Zealand was more important that being stubborn and staying outside for the sake of it. I crawled inside and slept on the sofa in a nice warm room for the remainder of the night. Aside from the obvious glaring mistakes that I made, the kit test had been a reasonable success and I felt confident in it getting me from North to South without any major hitches.

Do......

Time flies when you are in your last few weeks before a big challenge. And so it was the case in the weeks leading up to departure for The Gathering and then New Zealand. With a stretch of nights at work before this, it ensured that I was high on lack of sleep as much as anything else. But the time was fast approaching when I would have to turn all my dreams and words into deeds. Put my money where my mouth was. Last minute packing was fraught and made more complicated by the fact that I was taking my bike and some kit to The Gathering and I was going to have to be careful on my return that kit made it into the right places ready for my flight out.

There were nerves.. mostly because I was worried that I would let myself down by not being able to finish due to injury or another unforeseen event. Useless worrying really as my plans were detailed but ultimately flexible to cope with unexpected disasters (hopefully).

Little did I know that just getting to the airport would be a big enough challenge!

What follows is blogs from the road, kept as they were written at the time. The thoughts and feeling I express are honest to how I felt at the time. Following each blog will be my thoughts looking back on the experiences as I remember them now with additional comments. These are in *italics* to differentiate between then and now.

S#@t... F@*^.... B#@&*r

The day started well... no sign of the impending doom and disaster that was to befall me. Finished my night shift a bit early and raced home to get everything sorted that hadn't been sorted because of my seven day work stretch.

Currency picked up.. car packed... and bike on the bike rack... Half eleven... on the road to Wales for The Gathering pre flying off on Monday.

Tootling up the motorway ... no traffic... all good. I stopped off at Oxford services just to recheck the bike rack as you are supposed to do... all looking good.

Off onto the motorway again... love the M40.

The wind was gusting pretty bad and every now and again I had to fight the steering a bit. But all was going smoothly...

Until....

I felt the car being pulled back by the wind... then it settled. I glanced in my rear view mirror and in slow motion... I saw the back wheel of my bike drop a little... then settle... then tumble from my car and bounce behind me down the middle lane! Couldn't quite take the whole scene in... it's not a regular occurrence. I could see a lorry move slightly to the left as it manoeuvred round my now still bike...

Time stopped standing still suddenly and I pulled over to the hard shoulder... plan b... c... d...x rattling through my thoughts in the time it took for me to slow to a standstill..

Hazards on and then ... well what to do next?

I shakily dialled 999... haven't done that before (today a day of firsts)... and they assured me someone would be along shortly and advised me to hop over the barrier and wait there. I did as instructed and looking back down the motorway could see my lovely new shiny bike.. now with a wheel in the air. It didn't appear to be in bits at least but a new bike (again) was surely the order of the day. Perhaps there was a bike shop in Llandudno.

In no time at all I saw a Police van draw up on the hard shoulder and the policeman get out and retrieve my wounded bike. He drove up the hard shoulder and asked with a grin 'is this yours?'

As he wheeled my bike out a quick glance told me a lot... the frame miraculously was intact... the wheels appeared not to be buckled (how the hell did that not happen) The front tyre was flat and the rear mech appeared to be bent into the spokes... but it was in one piece (again... how the hell did that happen)

I explained to the policeman what I was doing.. where I needed to be.. and above all... why I needed to fix my bike asap. He suggested a nearby Halfords but on seeing the look of disgust on my face.. then suggested a 'proper' bike shop in Bicester.

We ascertained that it probably wasn't the best idea to tie my bike onto the rack and he offered to take my bike and let me follow him to the bike shop. What a fantastic bloke.

Ten mins later I was standing in the middle of the bike shop in Bicester... explaining what had happened... could they PLEEEAAASSSE fix it now.??

So up it went onto the stand and inspection ensued. Cost??? Didn't ask... didn't care. All I knew was... if they couldn't fix it... i was buying a bike on the spot... because come hell or high water (Alarm fans- see what I did there😃) I was going to The Gathering... my bike would be in a box on Sunday night and it would be on the plane Monday morning!

The good news... it's not your rear mech... it's the mech hanger (a lot cheaper part... good spot Mark Davies☺)

The bad news... we don't have one in stock! B#@@*r!

They then proceeded to phone round and found another bike shop 20 minutes away. I hopped in the car and sped (carefully) away. Meanwhile my brain is still trying to compute what has happened and above all work out how to get my bike from Bicester (if they fix it) to n wales.

I ran into the second bike shop ... got the mech hanger... and ran out again. Quite why i was in such a hurry when if they could fix the bike... it would mean at least two hours!

When I got back... a closer inspection revealed why the bike had fallen. Simply put... the bike rack had had a total and catastrophic failure of the straps holding the bike... they had simply split in half. So at least it wasn't due to incompetence or lack of care on my part... it did still leave me with the small problem of needing a way to carry my bike.

Back in the shop...

So .. do you sell bike racks??

£120 later.. I was in the possession of a very nice bike rack and they kindly fitted it onto my car too (not taking any more chances.)

Back in the shop... the good news is... (uh oh)

Your back wheel is fine...

The bad news is... your front wheel has a slight pinch point in the rim (i.e the rim is bent) ... new wheel then!

The handlebars were also damaged ... but the aero bars had survived... along with my bike computer (how the hell... Again!)

New bars meant new bar tape.... choices of colour and padding... hmmmmm what colour to have???

Whilst the rear mech hanger ... the wheel... the tyre... the handlebars... the gear cables... and (nope that was it) were being replaced.. I stood and chatted with the three mechanics. They asked about this ride... we discussed gear ratios and mountain bikes and advantages of 29er over 29+ and other crazy adventure plans and actually it was a very pleasant couple of hours ... given the circumstances 😄

Then came the worst bit... the bill. Prices were entered into the till and the amount of time it took to tot up gave an indication that this would be more than the price of an AMT coffee or two.

This is where Im going to name drop the bike shop....
Broadribb Cycles in Bicester... thank you so much... you have saved my next four weeks!
The cost of labour (extensive I might add) was slashed by 50% and a little money knocked off the cost of a couple of parts. Very kind to be sure. And this is the result....

And as you know... a glass is always half full... and every cloud has a silver lining and they are as follows...

No one got hurt (top of the list)

Somehow .. my frame and most of my bike was undamaged.. in fact my frame literally did not get one scratch.

As pointed out to me by one of the bike shop chaps... at least it didn't happen on the way home (Sunday evening... no bike shops open... flight Monday morning) which would have meant me purchasing a bike in Auckland - far from ideal

It cost me less than a new bike

I still got to N wales for The Gathering and my bike will be in a box on Sunday night... and on a plane Monday morning

I have shiny new blue bar tape - this alone makes the glass half full!!

I kept my saddle as although damaged... it now has character....

Fittingly... I wrote this below on my bike before I left this morning....

A good omen for the ride to come?
Could well be.
LHS

Yes.. it was a bit of a disaster but one that was easily sorted out in the end...

Good preparation for coping with any disasters that may befall me on the road.. Keyword... DON'T PANIC!

Watching my bike bounce down the middle lane of the M40 has become one of those stories told with a huge grin on my face... it's not often you get to recount a tale like that. I did have a slight worry that this signalled the shape of things to come.

The fact that my bike came out of its brush with destruction remains no small miracle to me.

It's the unexpected that you have to be prepared to deal with... clearly I was not planning to have to mend a broken bike 3 days before I was due to leave. All good plans have flexibility built into them, and then a plan b... c.. and so on. But that is what contributes most to the feeling of adventure on journeys such as I undertake. The knowledge that I have me and me alone to rely on and to come up with a solution. There is also the knowledge that you have to deal with the consequences of your choices, actions or general stupidity, as I was to learn later with good effect.

Day 0
95 RPM

Im currently sitting on my sofa... its 01:45... and it's also Day 0... D-day...

Ive been up now for around 18 hours having had next to no sleep the entire weekend and Im totally wired

Sentences form in my brain which dont make sense when I utter them aloud.... half thoughts that have fractured in my head floating round...

This day has been over two years in the making. With not much else to do but think as I pedalled from Chicago to L.A.. the seed was sown ... plans have been made.. and now is the time for action.

Dream... Plan... Do.

Events in my life have conspired in the last few months to feel lost... without direction or purpose.. everything shattered into pieces. A feeling with which I am not comfortable with and that unsettles me further... kinda like a snowball starting at the top of a mountain and gaining momentum as it rolls down the slopes... picking up more disquiet as it goes and heightening the lost feeling.

This is where it stops...

Cycling a challenge like this makes the mind and soul free. The necessity of focusing all energy and attention on the things important to mental and physical survival leaves very little room for anything else. All thinking effort is put into answering questions such as... 'will I get to where I want to be by the end of the day?' or shall I stop for food now or in 20 miles time? Have I got enough water to last me the day.? Will my legs last the day... or crumble under the pressure of the third 10 mile climb of the morning... and the big unanswered question.. Will I make it to the end?   All important questions to answer. This means that all the other shitty life problems.. big or small just sit floating in the back of the mind... organising themselves... with little or no help ... until they are sorted in alphabetical order and put the right way up (Donna and Simon!!) to be viewed at leisure.

This is why I like cycling long distances in short spaces of time - bike therapy in action!

I also like having a focus in my life... something to work towards...

My friends who know me well would just say its because Im crazy !

Whatever the reason... it has led me here... my sofa.. now 02:18 ... nerves jangling (though that may have been the large amount of caffeine I have consumed this evening)... bike in the box... rest of kit packed (bar the electricals to charge my phone and Ipod) and trying to sort out checking in.. photos from the weekend... and other small things .. on a computer that is sooo slow tonight of all nights... that I reckon I could cycle to New Zealand quicker than it is loading my email page.

The Gathering weekend... as always... was a crazy wonderful soul uplifting and emotional few days. And it is here that I want to thank Mike and Jules, James, Smiley, Mark and Craig for providing us with our yearly January blues beater ... all my Alarm friends for their support of the ride and for friendship formed from (not pure innocence this time) a shared love of life and the music of the Alarm ... and most of all thank the ones who have helped slow the snowball down.

The Gathering is hard to explain to those who have never been....

The conversation goes something like this...

So you are going away for a weekend in N Wales...?

Yup....

In January....?

Yup....

To see just one band...?

Yup!

At this point a somewhat incredulous look passes over their faces and there is a slight shake of the head.. and then as if to clarify...

N Wales in January?

As I reversed my car out of its parking slot... another Gathering done.. (roll on G25).. I put on my Ipod, which has been pre-filled with songs (have a guess as to which musician features highly) that I will be listening to as I sweat up the mountain passes... the song that came on first was not an Alarm or Mike Peters song... but Louis Armstrong... What a wonderful world. .. perfect song to describe at that moment how the Gathering had made me feel. Grateful to be part of The Alarm/LHS family and an overwhelming feeling of peace and tranquility.

It didn't last long... another 5 hours on the road ... followed by the sound of me revving up to 95 rpm.....

PART 2

Enough of the waffle.. I have a plane to catch and a challenge to start!

Practicalities....

(30 rpm)

The drive home was a long one... partly because I was crawling along at 60.. fearful of another bike rack road incident which my poor sleep deprived nerves could not have coped with. A short detour to hug my work mother... followed by a hug for my actual mum and dad... followed by a trip to work to hug my other work mother... oh and I forgot the detour to drop my brother off to pick up his van.

(40rpm)

So we arrived outside my house faced with a long list of jobs... and it was already 22:30. I got mice out of the freezer to defrost for snake feeding whilst simultaneously starting to haul off my lycra .. worn for bike ride promotional purposes at the Gathering.. (quick question Mike/Jules... am I the only person to have turned up to the Gathering in lycra??).

Balancing on one foot... holding my bike in one hand and mice in the other clearly wasn't going to work and It dawned on me that a more organised approach may be necessary...

We unpacked the car in short order and then Paul made the fatal mistake of lying down on my sofa...
Meanwhile I sorted out repacking my bags with the kit I had been wearing ... exchanging them for my 'off the bike clothes'. Once that had been accomplished... it was time to cross my fingers... find a four leafed clover ...beg the gods of plane baggage to keep my kit safe.. and put my bike in the box.
Being slightly tired by now... I did this in a somewhat arse over tip manner... taking off the front wheel before the pedals (makes it a bit trickier) .. putting bubble wrap and foam protectors over the vulnerable parts of the bike before ensuring it would fit in the box first. Despite all this kerfuffle.. between us we dissembled the bike (or is it disassembled.. Im not sure) slid it into the box where it sat looking like it was the perfect fit.. and then proceeded to throw in (I mean place with careful precision) the rest of my kit that I was not carrying as handheld. I knew that my seat pack would have to go separately .. but with the bike went my helmet... my bike shoes... the

29

bivvy pole... the frame bag the top tube bags and my shorts that I decided to wear over my cycling shorts (has pockets.. always good.).

(45rpm)
Triple check that all the components that I had taken off the bike... and the tools that I had used to do so... were all in the box. Pedals.. seat post and saddle and front wheel skewer were bubble wrapped and taped into the box.. followed by my pedal wrench. Tape the box shut... with as much tape as possible.. write fragile on it enough times that the baggage handlers get that it is fragile and then cross fingers that the bike ends up in the same part of the world at the same time as me... I have no contingency plan!

(60rpm)

Check in for the flight on the aforementioned slow as a tortoise computer.. which has very narrowly survived having something thrown at it! Only problem is .. due to my lack of patience (approaching 20 hours up) and my slow computer.. printing the boarding passes was One step farther from home than I could manage and so I gave up that idea and turned to putting up a few photos from the Gathering. ...

65rpm
MANY expletives later.....

70rpm
... It was approaching 0300 which meant it was time to wake Paul up (difficult) .. continue to try to be patient with my computer (impossible) and pack my handheld rucksack.
This was accomplished with the minimum of fuss and although I had to leave behind the water bladder... as it was a toss up between that and having a bit of space for food... (I figured I get several hundred separate slaps if I didn't leave room to carry a bit of food)...
Paul eventually dragged himself up and we proceeded to load the van.. with a few checks of passport and money.

80 rpm

It seemed no time at all that I was stepping out the door... suddenly a bag full of nerves... 2 years planning coming to fruition. Given all that had befallen my bike so far (fell off my car onto the M40 for anyone who hadn't read the blog entitled S$#&e.. F*$#.. B*$$#r) ... I think Im going to be a little more nervous until I am reunited with my bike.

95rpm

Traffic free roads ensured a speedy passage to the airport and a last minute dodging of the height restricted parking meant Paul had to go to the Drop off area instead of short stay parking. So abandoned to negotiate the check in with a very unwieldy trolley after the parting words of "For F$@* sake EAT" (Love ya bro) I made my way through check in over to outsize baggage drop where I watched in horror as the baggage handler proceeded to KICK.... YES KICK my bike onto the conveyor belt! You should have seen the expression on my face!!

He certainly did.. because he told me that I had seen nothing. Protesting loudly that I had indeed seen something (with a smile and a dagger at the ready) , he said if I had any complaints to put them in his colleagues name I think he was joking and it was actually all in good humour though I have visions of broken spokes and mech hanger issues. He wished me a nice day and we parted ways.

Next up... security! Damn Im good at this! Smugly having already removed everything from my pockets .. taken off watch... belt pouch.. money wallet and in short ensured I had everything covered... they asked me to dig out my tablet ... which of course meant practically emptying the entire contents of my rucksack... EPIC FAIL!

I then followed my brothers tip and headed to 'EAT' to locate some breakfast..although in reality this probably qualified as dinner as well due to fact that I had now been up an inordinate amount of hours.

How do I feel?

Well my sixth wind has kicked in so I still feel a bit wired...

Nervous... on two counts...
Hoping my bike makes it to Auckland in one piece and secondly about making it to the end...

This is what happened to me before though and as soon as I started turning the pedals.. all the nerves disappeared.. leaving me free to concentrate on the task at hand.

I'm looking forward to the mountains.. the lakes.. the warmer weather and blogging about it all to share it with anyone who is interested.

(Engine malfunction)
One Chai Latte and some kind of wrap later I have that annoying post food slumping feeling and the brain is fast shutting down (emergency power only)

And so begins the journey...
No doubt it will contain some crappy days and some mishaps along the way but that's what makes a journey into an adventure.

Share the journey with me...
www.facebook.com/OneChallengeAtATime

Marvel in the scenery with me (Instagram)

Suffer the hills with me (Action -cam footage and live updates via the Periscope App - @OneChallenge)

Fight Cancer with me (www.justgiving.com/GoWithTheCrazy) (*For anyone reading this now the journey has finished - a donation can be made to Love Hope Strength via Just giving at* https://www.justgiving.com/lhsf *)*

LHS

The Gathering this year for me was a mixture of the usual ... friends, music and inspiration... and a sadness. I said goodbye to my phoenix (Dave Spragg), willing the world to let me come back and see him. He promised me that he would be here when I got back. As I tore myself away, those words echoing in my head, I think I knew deep down ... I think he knew.. that my best friend would not be here when I got back. It was the hardest thing I have done to turn away and leave although I knew my phoenix would be watching over me as I rode and that he would certainly slap me if I hadn't gone...

Mike Peter's lyrics 'Life can be so cruel and unkind' continue to echo in my head along with the memory of that moment and it is hard to sit here and write about it without tears flowing for the brave friend I lost but his spirit and inspiration is weaved into the journey that follows.

If anyone wants to read Dave's personal story on his cancer fight, it can be found at http://www.lovehopestrength.co.uk/2014/01/my-lhs-story-dave-spragg/

He embodied all that LHS means and the inspiration of his story echoes far and wide.

Day 1

And I'm burning up... burning up...burning up such a long way from home

Day 1- a dollar and a day late in blogging so apologies for that... all will be explained.

So as you saw my brother abandoned me at the airport and I got through security pretty swiftly. An uneventful boarding and takeoff and subsequent very dull 13 hour flight was mitigated by the couple, Bernie and Paula, who i was sitting next to. Turns out Paula was a site manager at a hospital which made for very interesting topics of conversation for a few hours.. Despite being totally wired I did manage 3 hours sleep which took the edge of the weariness.

The welcome from Singapore was one of pouring rain but at least warm outside.. shame I was in the freezing airport.

This is where it all began to go slightly wonky...
Swollen legs from the flight were the least of my worries as I had now developed a nasty cough... a sore throat... chills alternating with a fever and aching all over. As I left Singapore I felt worse and.worse. This had the bonus of knocking me out for practically the whole flight. I slept through breakfast.. turbulence and the landing!!!

Clearing customs wasn't too bad but there were a few nerve wracking moments when I realised I had to declare my gels.. my bike..(fortunately not muddy) and persuaded them that my tarp was nearly new and had no mud whatsoever.

Baggage claim... bike had arrived.. slightly beaten up but seemed ok. A few holes in box with gear leaver sticking out but hopefully no damage.

Walking into arrivals I saw a cheery face waving at me. Despite the late hour Mark had come to pick me up to stay at his and his wife Sue's house. A random act of kindness to a complete stranger. Obviously living by my embrace the randomness theory.

Apparently I was pretty pale and probably didn't look like someone who would be able to cycle 1500 miles. Hey ho. Time will tell.

The wave of heat was fantastic after the cold airports and as we drove out of Auckland.. chatting away.. it felt like me and mark were old friends.

Collapsed into bed at around 2am with the hope that tomorrow was a new day and I would feel a whole heap better
Thats all folks... a day and a dollar late with the blog ... . but HERE!!

Slightly wonky is an understatement - looking back I realise just how ill I was. I think the adrenaline of being in a new country and the start of my ride, coupled with a need not to be totally anti-social to Mark and Sue, kept me going. At this point I wasn't really considering the task that lay before me and the fact that how I was feeling was going to render it next to impossible. The fact was, I had no choice. My schedule was so tight and left very little room for error that I didn't even consider taking an extra day to recuperate. Plus I believe that often if you give in to feeling ill, that gives the bugs a chance to take hold and close their fingers around you. If your head tells your body that it is ok and can keep going, it often does what it's told!

I do laugh at the thought of what Mark and Sue might have thought on seeing me, coughing, spluttering and struggling to breathe. But to their credit, no eyelids were blinked and they assisted me unquestioningly in the path I had set myself.

Day 2
Transfer Day

We took some photos to mark the 'off' and then it was time to go... bike safely stowed INSIDE the car. No more bike rack incidents risked!

Our first stop was at this cafe on the waters edge and while we were waiting Sue took me across the road to their local beach (as you do).

The sun was shining, the sky was blue and the slight breeze was just about right. In short absolutely perfect weather... a far cry from the cold wet weather I left behind me in Reading.

The hills rose up on the far side of the water and it looked idyllic. If someone had said to me... 'you cant do your ride.. you have to stay here for four weeks' Im not sure I would have been very upset... it was that nice.

Alas no one did... so once again we hopped in the car and headed for the Cape. This was a chance for me to see some of the roads I would be cycling on... assess their safety... surface quality and gradient. Also to get an idea of amount of civilisation around and how much to stock up on for the days of riding.

Mark pointed out how one minute we would be amongst civilisation, then it would just stop as if someone had drawn a line and said no more building after that.

The few towns we did pass were reminiscent of small town America in their layout and signage and type of building which was a little surprising. There seemed to be enough places to eat along the roads and although sparse in places there would be enough places to stop and stock up on food and water and the like.

The road was of good quality with a decent shoulder most of the way. The bit Mark and Sue were worried about was a long winding climb with sharp bends but as far as I could see, the few cars we saw were driving sensibly and not haring it round the bends. After this there was even a long flat(ish) stretch which I could see my aero bars coming into play here. All in all it looked good and despite the climbs.. the stunning scenery would be enough to distract me. Hills and green brush for as far as I could see in every direction... unspoilt on the whole by man, with just the odd farm or campsite interrupting the endless green vista.

The journey was a long but very pleasant one with a myriad of subjects covered. Its weird how you can feel you know someone and just click. (Mark and Sue: you may disagree) and its here I would like to thank them both for embracing the randomness and going with the crazy (hopefully not fighting the fear this time) and helping out a complete stranger. Not everyone would do this and I am very grateful for both their help and for life causing our paths to cross.

We stopped for some lunch at a small town and although I really wasn't hungry, did my best to eat something. Mark disappeared off to the car whilst I finished blogging from the day before... trying to keep you all updated.

The rest of the journey passed uneventfully and as we came in to Kaitaia the plan was for Mark and Sue to check in to their motel .. we grab dinner... and then head up to Cape Reinga. As Sue was checking in... Mark said 'Im going to make a suggestion... I think you should stay in a motel tonight here (rather than camp up at the Cape) and then we can drive up in the morning.' Now normally my stubborn streak would kick in right about that moment... but the thought of a motel.. in my current state.. did sound pretty good. Bit unfair on dragging mark and sue up at some ungodly hour though as needed to set off by 8 am really... because the way I feel today means Im not going to be setting any speed records on the road tomorrow. As sue came back in the car.. I voiced my concerns about dragging them up early... all of which were quickly batted away. The voices of reason (Mark and Sue) outdid my stubborn streak very quickly and as me and sue went in to the hotel she said it was about $170. Slightly more than I had considered but needs must. There was a room available and as I got my monopoly money out to pay... the gentleman at the counter said that he would do me the room for just $60. Turns out Sue had already told him what I was doing and he kindly gave me a discount. How nice is that!!

So as I collapsed into a very nice motel room.. another coughing fit brought up what little I had eaten for lunch and left me feeling a bit washed out. The rest of the evening has been spent dozing and blogging. SPOT was activated but for some reason didn't register so Im trying again as we speak.

And so tomorrow it begins.... a little apprehensive still as always before starting something like this but once the wheels are turning it will all fall away leaving me and the road.

The phoenix will rise.. it might just take a day or so to reach full flight.
LHS

A huge thank you must once again go to Mark and Sue. They were introduced to me via the wonders of modern technology (Facebook) by a friend of mine. (Thank you Matt D) Despite not having a clue who I was and never having met me, they both immediately sent offers to help me in whatever way they could. When it became apparent that I was going to have difficulty in getting to the very North of the island with my bike, without hesitation, they offered to pick me up from the airport, have me stay with them and then drive a long way to deliver me to the starting point. The journey might never have started without this assistance and I remain forever appreciative of their kindness. In addition to that, their voices of reason at the beginning of the journey might well have saved the whole journey and their friendship calmed the nerves at the start of this challenge enabling me to focus on the road that lay ahead.

Day 3
Chewed up ... Spat out!

Well... how the hell do I describe today. Not sure of a title for this blog yet but it may become clear as I lay out e v e r y painful step of Day 3.

Firstly and without further ado... I wish to reintroduce myself to you.. for today at least... as dumb f#@$€r and while I struggled to find a word that wasn't a swear word... I gave up as nothing else seemed appropriate. Rest of that story later.

You may remember from yesterday's blog that the voices of reason (Mark and Sue Hobbs) had persuaded me that it was a good plan to stay the night in a comfy motel and they weren't wrong. A reasonable nights kip... waking a few times... before an early start in order to get up to the Cape.

Before I knew it we were there. Weirdly we were there. And as we walked down to the lighthouse it all seemed a bit too real. We took photos and as I stared out to the two oceans meeting (not the only place you can see this!) I realised that once again I myself would be subject to the whim and force of nature. Rarely benevolent... occasionally uninterested.. but always around you. I feel that when I'm on my bike... the sheer insignificance.

This feeling was compounded somewhat when I got on my bike.. made to cycle off for a photo shot and... crash! Brakes had jammed the wheel causing me to go flying and scrape a bit of skin off my knee. Great start!

There was little time for pontificating though... I had to leave... and I had to go soon. I had been faffing to delay the inevitable cutting the cord moment between myself, Mark and Sue. Clinging on to what you know.. even if not for very long. Hugs all around... a promise to stay safe (note no promise not to be a dumb f#$@*r) .. music in the ears and off I went (again).

The first small section was downhill and after that the first 20 miles are a bit of a blur. Firstly.. breathing is an issue today. Im pretty short of breath and I take a deep breath I cough my guts up and thats almost no exaggeration. So there I was literally wheezing past the most beautiful scenery and I could not quite show the appreciation it deserved. Snot (apologies for those sensitive of stomach... I'm afraid it gets worse..) was literally pouring out of me and my hacking cough had me doubled up.. trying to quell both the cough and the feeling of being about to throw up. A portable suction catheter wouldn't have gone amiss.

That aside.. it was pretty hot.. and I was getting through water like there was no tomorrow. Which was another concern. Anyhow .. I plodded on...

At some point amongst the plodding I started to take note of my surrounding. Reminiscent of Cornwall... Wales... and states such as Missouri (the hills.. oh the hills) and Oklahoma (the sidewind .. oh the sidewind). Even on the downhill I was battling... not to go forward .. but at the very least not to go sideways. The sand dunes gave way to chalk and dense bush was something to behold in places. At one point.. I stopped.. took out the earphones and listened to cacophony of sound emanating from it. Crickets and birds whistling their own tune of life.

By now I was becoming mildly concerned about several things. Firstly.. the time... it was a ticking and I was not going very fast. Second water running out... and third .. my right shoe was not unclipping... a problem I had had in America. I had spare cleats so just needed to stop somewhere and fix it. The problem I had was I stopped on a hill.. with one foot permanently clicked in. There was nothing for it but to remove foot from said shoe.. walk up the hill with one shoe.. coast down the other side and find a place in shade where I could sort stuff.

A solution came in the form of a motel/ b and b where the owner kindly let me fill my water bottles and fix my shoe..

Easier said than done of course as I couldn't get the bloody thing off the pedal. Almost at the point of despair 15 mins later... I tugged really hard... caught my fingers on the chain ring.. gouging out skin.. but victoriously holding the shoe. Once free it was quickly fixed. Smiling at what today was throwing at me I pedalled onwards.. coughing fits punctuating the air as I wound up and down.

The terrain was still pretty unforgiving but in the back of my head I knew it flattened out a bit before Kaitaia... where exactly I wasn't sure but the thought kept me grinding up the mountains.

The scenery when I noticed it had changed into pasture filled with horses and cattle. Surprisingly I didn't see many sheep.

I had also determined that to get to Kaitaia would be probably a stretch too far and alternative plans had run round my head... stop short and make it up another day being the foremost one at this point. Having relaxed a bit about my destination I decided to sit down by the roadside and eat a few of the provisions I had obtained. Some goddam awful salami thing, nuts and a banana and chocolate flapjack (One of your five a day). I sat there opposite this very picturesque gate which appealed to my picture taking side of me. I then sat there in peace and tranquility watching some bird of prey wheel over the hill, and then Breathe came on my Ipod(a Mike Peters song for those of you who don't know) and the scene was complete. It was a perfect moment in an otherwise difficult day.

Half an hour gone, I got up, hopped back on the bike and freewheeled down the road, the much anticipated flat part coming up. Even getting down onto the aero bars for a bit, my brain started thinking about the possibility of getting to Kaitaia as planned. I was still having difficulty breathing however and the next stop brought on a coughing spasm which saw the aforementioned salami end up on the road. Nice!

I passed some nice flowers that I almost took a picture of but decided to plod on, and didn't stop again till I screeched to a halt at a sign for Salvation Road (dead end lol) and reached into my pocket to get my phone. Now you remember I introduced myself as dumb f$#@*r, well here's why. I scrabbled around in one pocket, then the other as it it slowly dawned on me that my phone was most definitely not there. Call it the final straw for today but I was not smiling any more. In fact I was very angry with myself. In my desperation, I rang Mark, (on the other NZ phone he had given me) in the hope he would be in the area. To his great credit, he didn't blink a eyelid - least not that I could tell over the phone. He was over two hours away and was considering driving back to take me back up the road to go find it. At which point my stubborn, angry, stupid self finally came to my senses and told him not to worry, I'd just turn round and go back. I was pretty certain it was by the gate, where I'd eaten cos I hadn't stopped since then. He said to hang on and he would call back in a few minutes. When he rang back he had an idea of phoning around his police buddies to see if there was a patrol car that could take me back to where I dropped it. Those few minutes sitting by the roadside however had hardened my resolve. My mistake, therefore my punishment.

I thanked him and turned my bike round to start the pedal back towards the gate. It couldn't have been that far right? Frankly it felt like ten miles but was probably only 5 max and as the gate drew into view, my fingers were firmly crossed that It would be there. I crossed the road, leaned the bike against the embankment and began a systematic sweep of the area I thought it would be in. Not there! Just as I was beginning to despair, I walked a little further, certain in my mind that I wasn't sitting this far up, when suddenly I noticed my phone, lying nonchalantly on the ground. I could hardly believe my luck. I texted Mark to let him know the good news before, once again, turning my bike around and heading in the direction I was supposed to be going.

I was dead on my feet and frankly had decided pretty much to stop at the first motel available. Back to where I realised my phone was missing, I took a photo of the Salvation road sign, aware that if it hadn't stopped me I wouldn't have known the phone was gone. Salvation indeed!!. A few more mins down the road an advert for

45

food and accommodation jumped out and I wheeled down the gravel track. It all looked a bit shut but as I turned round to head back to the road, a voice asked if she could help.

Now whether it was my general broken state, or the fact that whenever I tried to talk, with my now defunct voice, I collapsed in spasms of coughing, I'm not sure, but something brought out a motherly instinct in this lady I'd just met and within minutes, I'd been shown to a lovely wooden cabin, ushered onto a sofa, given hot honey and lemon, and some for an overnight flask, as well as a very nice meal of 'snapper' fish with salad, some fruit for tomorrow and an offer of a herbal remedy to open the lungs as I was still short of breath. I was then charged for the room only, free meal and sundries, so very kind! So a massive thank you to Helen and Russel of the Houhora tavern for being my saviours today.

I collapsed in my cabin and assessed the damage of the day.

I felt like I had been chewed up and spat out on the road today and my headspace is not good. A short hop into Kaitaia with a rest day was one idea but my phoenix is telling me to shut up and get on with it tomorrow, so will do my utmost. I hope I have the strength to continue forward motion come what may.

So that was Day 3. What an introduction!

Perhaps its too early for this song quote but it feels apt...

It's alright, It's ok.....

LHS

P.s - apologies of lack of replies to messages and comments. I will try to answer all in the morning, but thank you everyone for the support x

Reading this back a few months later- I firstly realise how careless I was, leaving my phone on the side of the road. It was my lifeline in a way that I had discovered out on Route 66. Previously I had thought of myself as the sort of person who could just ride off into the wilderness for months on end with no connection to the outside world. Turns out that this is not the case as I break out in a bit of a cold sweat when I think of the lifeline family and friends provided me via the medium of Facebook, twitter and other 21st century inventions. Lifeline in that the support and encouragement kept me sane when my sanity was attempting to fly over the mountain pass before me and disappear.

This was a disappointing revelation for me but having accepted it, to then leave my mode of communication on the roadside had indeed put in the category of 'stupid f$@%$r'.

I will admit here now - and apologies to Helen and Russell but I had no intention whatsoever of taking a herbal remedy. People who know me will know that I have to be force fed pills if I'm ill and if I can get away without I most certainly will. i am a even more distrustful of herbal remedies. However the kindness and concern in their every offering was unparalleled and at the moment when i needed it most - kindness was showered upon me and for that I will be eternally grateful.

For those that aren't avid followers of The Alarm, Breathe is one of the most beautiful songs ever and is one of those that will cause the hairs to stand up on the back of your neck. I love listening to it when I'm at the top of a mountain, or on the road with nothing but open space in front of me. The lyrics reflect in part, how I feel at these times when I ride along the 'black highways'.

Silver rivers reflect the sun
On black highways I will be done
Mile on mile of empty heat
I will wait for you…
I will not look back
Chasing shadows all night long
Indian nation… a tattooed arm
Manifest destiny drives my car
I will follow you…. I will not look back
I breathe the air
I watch the sun
Rise and fall
In twenty four hours
I breathe

Day 4
It is this that will define me

Following being fussed over last night I managed some sleep and woke up this morning with a somewhat better outlook on life despite the howling wind whistling around the walls of my cabin. The coughing was still there but the shortness of breath had improved and I thought to the words of a friend... pedal like fcuk today. And indeed thats what I intended to try and do.

My aimed for start time of half 7 became 8, as I pottered around, trying not to cough, ate a breakfast bar, drank some more honey and lemon and then proceeded to make myself 'weather proof'. The blacks swans had come in from the lake - a sure sign of really bad weather. Out came the rain and wind jackets, the overshoes and into the bag went my gillet. Off the bike clothes were packed as I transformed myself into something resembling a cyclist. Double checking phones (maybe triple checking that one), passport and money.

Arse cream on and ready to go, when the realisation dawned that I needed a wee. No doubt all the fluids overnight coupled with the pattering of rain outside. This short trip involved an almost complete undressing and delayed my departure. As I looked towards the house I couldn't see any sign of movement so didn't get the opportunity to thank Russell and Helen again for their kindness.

The rain had now reached downpour levels and combined with a gusting side/head wind meant it was blasted into me at a rate of knots. The road was ok in terms of gradient with the kind of ups and downs I have already come to expect but my legs felt ok. The rest of my body hasn't quite caught up. Although not as bad as yesterday, I was still having difficulty breathing at times and every stop was interspersed with coughing fits. I was doing food and water better today, All I had to do was open my mouth for a few seconds and it would fill up in seconds with water from the sky... it was that wet!

My feet were already soaked but at least warm and although my legs and arms were wet my main trunk remained dry. Was just keeping my fingers crossed that Apidura bags lived up to their reputation. So far so good and first 15 miles covered ok. The sidewinds had required my utmost attention as they came blasting through the gaps and hit my bike with enough force to push me half way across the road. I have encountered this before and leaning at a 45 degree angle is the appropriate response. Of course this can change quickly when a car, lorry or wind break comes up and suddenly you are fighting not to topple unceremoniously into the ditch. Bet it all looks quite amusing actually and at points in this stretch, I was enjoying the battle, a bit of my phoenix emerging and encouraging me, a bit of my true self, and not the weak weary self that I seem to have brought to New Zealand. Encouraging signs for sure. But then doubts resurfaced and the next ten miles I spent in a great debate with myself (often aloud),but more of that in a bit.

In the meantime I had my first, second and third encounters with the world renowned Logging Truck. It was not overly pleasant. 2 trailers long, piled high with the load, it came thundering up behind me, signalling its intent of going fast and close with a rev of the engine. A blast of spray hit me first followed by the swirling current it created. To its credit, it had moved out slightly, but moved in too quickly for my liking, leaving me with the thought that the road space was running out. However, probably practiced at being an ar#$ h#@€, he just scraped past in time, leaving me to spit out road water and gain a modicum of control of my somewhat wobbly bike. The second and third encounters were better as I knew what to expect and pulled well over on to the shoulder, raised a hand in advanced thanks and held on tight. These two passed well around me and caused no problem. Sorted. These trucks are monsters and even when on the other side of the road create a big enough draft to disturb your course of travel.

The scenery now was greener with more dense brush, including a myriad of what only could be described as broccoli trees, as that is what they looked like. I cant claim credit for that description, it was what Mark had described them as on the way and it is uncannily accurate. I kept an out out for the famous Kauri trees and passed a place which advertised having them (8Km off route) with what was possibly a trunk of one of them outside. It was a pretty impressive trunk but not enough to make me detour to be fair, and may get another opportunity later on in the ride.

Back to the debate with myself. The sensible part of me was whispering that it was all about the long game. My aim is to arrive in Bluff on the 27th feb, and given my condition at the moment I could very well ground myself into the (wet) dust well before then if I didn't sort both my body and my head out.

I feel a shadow of myself at the moment (not asking for sympathy - just the way it is) and my head correspondingly is not playing ball. My head says go... go... go... my body says nope, nope, nope and then my head goes .. ok then. Its frustrating more than anything because my legs feel ok at the moment.

I am also aware that a lot of people have sponsored me to do this (thank you very much) and pride is very much as stake here.

Given all this, despite the whispering of my inner pride, I realised that Kaitaia was the furthest I should sensibly go today. With my head sorting through schedules and time, I decided to stop here, take the rest of the day as a rest day, and attempt to recuperate somewhat, with the long game in mind.

Whether it is the right decision, time will tell, as I may regret using a whole rest day up for only half a day and there may be a day further on where I need one more... but this is the game I choose to play. Assessing the situation and reacting as I see fit at the time. You can all mutter, told ya so later , and I might well agree but at this moment, it seemed to be the right idea, a notion reinforced by events shortly about to occur.

I rolled back up to the Orana motor inn, the one myself, sue and mark had stayed in on the first night up north. I didn't expect another discount but it would at least stop me having to explain why I had rocked up soaked through and out of breath! As I went through the door, a lady receptionist enquired what I wanted, and just as I dissolved into a coughing fit trying to explain, the guy who was there the first night walked through the door. He took one look at me, said 'don't worry we'll look after you' ushered me to a room said if there was anything I needed to let him know and when I asked about pizza in the area he offered to delay his own run into town whilst I got changed and then take me there and back. Bloody hell! Another injection of kindness from a stranger which is becoming less surprising the further I dip my toe into this country.

Peter, as it turns out his name was, is a brilliant chap who found me at a low ebb and helped pick me up. Faith in human kind given a bump up for sure!

And so began an afternoon of crap tv (Dr Phil anyone) and resting. I have discovered two massive bruises on my back, presumably where a plug has been digging in... thought it hurt!! Need to do something about that for tomorrow.

Then followed the live update... no film director me... and clearly should try and move my hand away from the camera... it seemed to work and added a bit of fun to my day. Hopefully other live updates will be outside in sunshine! If you missed it and want to catch up.. either find @OneChallenge on the periscope app or go to www.periscope.tv/OneChallengeAtATime

And so thoughts turn to tomorrow. I know I have a pretty stiff hill climb after leaving Kaitaia but then a bit of a downhill run. The weather isn't supposed to be great but needs must. Then its a ferry ride towards Oppononi. Sounds easy right☺

I will give it my all and fight to keep the pedals turning and hopefully take you all on the journey with me.

A massive thanks to my family and friends for all the support. It would have been a whole heap more miserable without it.

LHS as always for tomorrow I fight back!

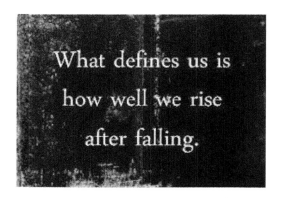

What defines us is
how well we rise
after falling.

It's funny how the memories of the awful weather on this day have faded. I do remember the extreme hassle of the process of going for a wee - blokes have it a lot easier for sure on this point.

An honourable mention for the Apidura bags must come here. They withstood the torrents of rain as well as I had hoped they would. Very well made and durable, it is no surprise that many ultra-racers choose them.

The Periscope App was an addition to my social media repertoire on this trip and it was a bit hit or miss due to the general lack of mobile signal available in many areas I ended up on. My main aim for this Periscope update was to show people that i was pretty sick, and not just moaning about a slight sniffle. It prompted one of my consultants at work to message me and advise I go find some antibiotics... (sorry Dr P - no time).

Re-reading this blog again - it shows me that the fight that I felt had deserted me, was still there and I was certainly determined not to be defined by failure to get going again in the morning. Oddly enough (given my general Fight The Fear statement), much of what kept me going was probably fear... fear of failing, fear of letting those who believed in me down, fear of not being as strong as I hoped I would be. So I guess that if fear drives you to push yourself and keep going, that kind of fear may not have to be fought, but embraced... in order to Go With The CraZy...

Unfortunately mostly fear drives people to run away, give up and that is the sort of fear that I will rail against until the day I die.

Day 5
My heart is starting to beat in the echo of the road

This morning seems a hugely long time ago. A whole week seems to have been crammed into the course of the day somehow.

It started when I left the comfort of the Orana motor inn in Kataia and headed out into a slightly drizzly dreary day. I felt better ... well than yesterday and my headspace was certainly more sorted for sure. I pottered along the road waiting for The Big Climb to appear. Now I had seen it from the car on the way up and several people had told me about it but nothing truly prepares you. But more of that in a bit. Today was humid warm... too warm for rainwear.. but there was rain... more drizzle today than the torrential of yesterday but also a welcome relief in many ways.

I said my headspace was better today... i think I've stopped trying to see the whole and concentrate on each day... and if necessary... breaking it into smaller pieces. So today was from Kaitaia.. up Mangamuka gorge (god knows how long that would take) ... down Mangamuka gorge (wooohoooo) - part 1 done. Part 2 from Mangamuka to the ferry and part 3 the ferry to Oppononi. Made it sound easier for sure.

As I approached the climb .. the scenery abruptly changed... seemingly in the blink of an eye. One minute it was rolling fields... the next ... 'jungle' so dense and full of sound it was reminiscent of Madagascar... and this occupied me nicely for the lower part of the climb. Rivers... waterfalls... the gorge ... stunning!!

Before I reached the actual climb... i was surprised to see not one.. but at least five lycra clad guys (yes they were on bikes).. ended up stopping to chat which was so nice as only cyclists can appreciate the terrain... that said I envied their unencumbered bikes. I was conscious of delaying their ride.. more than mine to be fair and suggested they go ahead.. because frankly it would have been very embarrassing. One of them suggested I fall in with them for a bit! Lol... the mere suggestion that even if well.. i could keep up with them.. even as a tail hanger.. was so funny it ended up in a coughing spasm (yup still having those). They wished me luck and I wished them a good ride and we went our separate ways...

Which left me v the gorge...and let me tell you... it was a climb and two thirds with only half my normal lung capacity. The first bit was ok ... frequent stopping still required but it was relentless. A bit like the steps in Switzerland bro... when you turn the corner and think you are there you are faced with another bend upwards. For the second half of it I was stopping most bends... generally cos i was so slow that i wanted to ensure no cars/lorries would go round that bend the same time as me. Fortunately there was hardly any traffic... so actually that just became an excuse to stop... cough up my guts .. try and breathe... summon the fortitude... mutter to myself that the top wasn't getting any closer just standing there.. and go again.

Eventually I got to the top... I asked a lady in a car coming the other way, to make sure I wasn't disappointed. Then came a long sweeping.. beautiful downhill which I will post as soon as I have better access to plug points.

It almost made up for all the struggle of the last three days... almost!

Then I headed towards Mangamuka... worried I would miss the turnoff and knowing I needed to eat soon.. I stopped at a cemetery (just because it had a place to lean my bike and a tap (apparently for hand washing before and after visiting) - used by me to fill water bottles... ate some disgusting protein bar and then continued onwards. I think it was about here that I became aware of a van driving up alongside me and the occupants saying something to me.. i pulled my headphones out and realised (with prompting) that it was one of the cyclists I was chatting to earlier. He asked how I was... whether i needed anything. Such absolute kindness again shown to me by a not so complete stranger (this being the second time we had met). So thank you Roger... it was a pleasure to meet you. LHS

Just down the road.. I found a hot bacon and cheese toastie and decided it would be rude not too ...

Next up ferry... and as I took the turn... upwards of course... I felt pretty good with the day so far. I realised I might make the two pm ferry and the road whilst winding up and down... wasn't too bad.

Miles and miles later..
I rolled into town at 13:52 ... only to find that the ferry left from 4Km down the road... i 'leaped' onto my bike and hotfooted it. It was a loong four k and I pulled into the ferry terminal at 14:04 to have to watch the ferry sail untroubled away. Bummer! Still an enforced hours rest ... in a beautiful spot... who am i to complain... especially as I had been aiming for the 15:00 ferry anyway.

An hour later I rolled my bike on... and ended up chatting to the deckhand Jack and his friend.. self- confessed layabout.. Jock. Jack even offered me an apple (yes I did accept and ate it on the spot). Nice guys and we passed the journey chatting away.

Off the ferry... a steep climb up.. then nice until turned onto SH12 and my new road to follow for a while. It was up and down .. though felt more like up but to cut a hilly story short I crawled into my days destination, Oppononi, at around 5pm.

Then it was all business. No rooms at any inn so bivvy it was and I did have fun setting up around the goats. Wasn't wholly keen on bivvying it tonight as still feel pretty rough but needs must and actually it's stopped raining and is warm.

My final story for today is of a pot noodle dinner (all the cafe's closed) rescued by the unexpected kindness of my tent neighbours (I was upset about them pitching so close to my bivvy).

One of the young girls came in to where I was blogging and offered me two sausage sandwiches on a plate with a glass of juice. Once again bowled over by the generosity and care of strangers.

And that is a good place to leave todays blog... so I'm going to tuck myself in to my sleeping bag and try and rest for tomorrow it begins again...

Today my heartbeat started to echo that of the road.
Nn everyone LHS To you all

Looking back over day 5 - in my memory it was one of the nicest days of them all. It was the first day where I had felt more like a reasonably competent cyclist, I was beginning to feel a bit better and the countryside itself had transformed into one which made me feel like I was finally in a foreign country. The noise of the insects was all pervading and provided an ongoing soundtrack. (NB - this is before the bloody things started biting me!)

It felt like a tropical paradise and the sounds, sights, and smells distracted me for the main part from the effort of breathing. It was also the site of my first proper climb and subsequent descent. I do remember being slightly tentative on the descent and not taking full advantage because of the unfamiliar roads and the hairpin turns made slick in the drizzle.

The Ferry - whilst I could have very well been annoyed at missing it - it led to an enjoyable hour of sitting on a bench with my bike next to me, feeling totally free. As cars pulled up one by one to wait for the next one, the occupants made me laugh. I don't think one of them got out of their car for more than a minute - and that was to run over to the toilet block! They were in front of a beautiful lake, surrounded by trees and greenery, could have filled their lungs with fresh air and filled their hearts and souls with the essence of the country. Instead they sat glumly in their metal boxes - barely talking to any other occupants. It made me feel very privileged to be aware of all the things that they missed

By the time I got to the Oppononi- I have to admit that I was pretty devastated to have to camp but in the end it was a very cool experience (and one I'm going to have to get used to for future adventures). I will usually jump at an opportunity to get my tent out but in this case I was knackered and still feeling ill - slightly worried about how I would feel in the morning after a night under the stars. Turns out that it was a beautiful night, the wind blowing ever so gently through my bivvy, but not enough to disturb the cosy shelter I had built myself.

It was on this day that the rhythm of the road and being linked to it began to echo through me. It's like everything else disappears and all you can feel is the tarmac under your wheels, the feel of the wind, rain and sun on your skin - becoming lost in the world around and the feelings it pulls out of your senses and instills them deep inside your soul. It's hard to describe but you know it when you get there and I wish for everyone that I know that they will one day feel it too. There is pain and discomfort in this world too but all but the most severe discomfort becomes part of the greater whole, part of the feeling and it all becomes one within you, strengthening and forging a new part of you that may one day be called upon in tougher times.

Day 6
Living on a Knife Edge

My day started with a buzzing in my ear. Nope it wasn't the mosquito that had been annoying me all night but my watch alarm telling me it was 5am and time to get stuff squared away. Why so early... well when you've bivvied.. ideally you want stuff to be dry-ish and it takes a long time to get all the kit squared away in my morning routine... even without the camping kit.

The night had passed peacefully enough. My bivvy was perfectly set up and when it did rain.. I heard the patter of raindrops on my tarp but didn't feel a drop. It was actually pretty snug under there. I had been very warm as well as totally dry... pretty comfortable (no hip pain bro) and aside for a couple of coughing fits had slept bloody well. The odd spider had of course found its way towards me overnight and I shook several off me as I got up.

The biggest nuisance had been the flies buzzing round my face until my headtorch had been extinguished and then went to find some other poor bugger to bother. I also discovered a wasp taking shelter (well if you do set up a bloody good shelter you should expect others to take advantage)

So I started packing up... dragging all my stuff to the campsite kitchen area to lay out before packing up. I had the whole place to myself as it still wasn't light... laying out wet kit... using the benches to spread out my camping kit and generally make myself at home. It seemed to take ages to sort everything.. in fact almost 2 hours and as I rolled my bike out to the exit .. I was annoyed with myself for taking so long.

Just as I was about to saddle up.. the reception man came out and started asking me about LHS. Inwardly groaning slightly cos I needed to get on the road, but mindful that a big part of this journey for me is spreading the word and getting others involved. Once I'd given him the lowdown.. he wished me luck and gave me 10$ for the charity. How nice was that!! And worth the ten minutes chatting to him for sure.

My departure could be delayed no longer... I had to find food. The pot noodle (I had bought 2 last night) was donated to a better cause than my stomach - the bin- and I had nothing except a few cereal bars on me. Down the road I went... away from Oppononi towards Dargaville - my eventual destination. The road ran along the beach and the morning sun lit up the water and the golden sand dunes making them unspeakably perfect in that moment.

Enough admiring the view -said New Zealand - lets see how she copes with this!! Now as I discovered in my little jaunt across America.. the first ten miles of the day will always HURT anyway... throw in a hill - by hill Im talking mountain by English standards - shut the cafe thats just before the the start of it and what do you get... one teetering wobbly shell of the person you may know as Lydia, Lid, crazy girl.

It went straight up. The tarmac was of the kind that seemed to hold the wheels in place... so much so I was convinced my brakes had jammed on and kept checking them for a problem. Crawling on my knees would have been quicker for me to get up there. I kept stopping and taking an age to contemplate moving again. (Still a couple of gut wrenching coughing fits just to dig the knife in) It was a hell of a downer right off the bat. This was just the first little lump in the road of what I was sure was going to be many today and it was taking too long. My slightly fragile mind was already stressing about getting to my destination that day... calculating time/distance as it would do for the rest of the day. Even though it seemed a bit early in the day for 'hike a bike' there was a stretch I got off and walked simply because a hill start was not possible.. such was the angle of the road.

Crap crap and crap... i was frustrated... my thoughts turning to failure and letting everyone down. I eventually reached the top but the seeds were sown and throughout the day would creep back in uninvited.

I did of course eventually reach the top and as I turned round and leant on my aero bars (seeing my pain is weakness leaving the body quote) ... the view was unbelievable. In a very short space of mileage I had gained a huge amount of altitude and I could see across the stretch of water, whipped by the wind into a teeming mass of white topped waves, to the impossibly tall sand dunes. Just visable was a section of rainbow to top off the picture postcard moment. It held my gaze for a while and as it did Mike's song Breathe came around on my Ipod with impeccably good timing.

Couldn't stand around for long though... I had breakfast to find (you see Im trying to eat!!)

I raised the gears out of 'granny mode' and turned my bike down the other side...
Speedy downhill right? Nope .. still felt like I was peddling through treacle... what the hell was wrong????

Fortunately a short hop downhill found an open cafe and an impossibly large breakfast of eggs bacon beans and sausage along with a banana smoothie! Very nice and I sat there chilling for 5 when it walked three helmeted lycra clad women who informed me they were admiring my bike. Really?? But Ive transformed it into a beast of a bike... far from its clean sleek race-lines. Then I looked at their bikes.. Mountain bikes with similar set up for carrying kit as me yet they still exclaimed over how little I was carrying for the ride I was doing. They were kinda doing the same thing... only in race format.. and their ride would be mainly off road. Known as the Tour Ateroa (hope spelled correctly) it is a self supported race from top to bottom... interesting!

Anyway eventually got back on the road and food had made my legs feel much worse. If I was in treacle before... I was now tethered to the road... so slow was my progress.. up/down/flat made little difference and I was just about to throw all my toys out of the pram.. when 2 unencumbered cyclists approached from behind - with a lot more speed- and informed me of the road ahead. Specifically... some downhill after the Kauri tree.. then a bit of up.. but the last 40Km's into Dargaville were all downhill and with that they whizzed off.. leaving me eating their dust.

this is a long one....

The road to the beginning of the Waipura forest was up and down and sapped all my energy and gave fuel to my levels of rising despair. Despite this I managed to look around and appreciate the country I was suffering through. Green pastures all around.. dotted with trees and fences. It could have been England.. or Wales... and bits reminded me of Italy. Until I reached the forest. Madagascan jungle foliage closed around the road.. the birds and crickets continuing their never ending chorus. It just switched... like that! With the jungle came the up. Very similar to the Manganuka gorge I went through yesterday in terms of up and bend.. more up and bend in a never-ending parody of itself. And there was me... a small dot struggling up it. Within this forest lay my first goal of today. The Kauri tree... specifically the biggest known living one. It was another hour and a half of uphill grind before a quick descent to the visitors centre. A climb which drove me to the edge as it just felt like there was far too much resistance to the wheels going forward. Treacle tarmac again. So much so I had to pedal the downhill section or I would have stopped.

I pulled in and followed others across the road to the walkway that led to THE tree. The jungle calmed me... immersed in the sounds and smells of nature brought my mind back to sense again and I marvelled at the tangled vines and the dense undergrowth. And then there was the tree. And yes it was big... but that wasn't it. Held as sacred by the Maori .. you can feel why. It emanated permanence where all around was change. Things lived and died around it and it continued .. unmoved. I felt in awe in the true sense of the word. And it was just a tree. Maybe because next to it.. we all dwarf into insignificance.

Difficult to describe but I left exceptionally glad I had stopped and seen it. Much better than a man made 'worlds biggest'. I then got ripped off for tap water to refill my bottle... just to bring me back to ground level.

The following descent was on better tarmac and swept past more ancient Kauri trees.. not as big in stature but impressive nonetheless. I counted about 15 that I swept past... not quite Sean Kelly (Irish Cyclist) but not bad for someone on a loaded bike on damp roads (did I mention more rain) which contain cars!

The rest of the day was spent awaiting that 'all downhill into Dargaville' that the cyclist told me this morning. As I met them on their way back... they were probably going oh shit.. now she has worked out we were lying. With the reply of ' but it gave her something to look forward to throughout the day'. There was some down... but it was not the equal of the up and each up was a granny gear grind. These ups I'm referring to... whilst not like the Mangamuka gorge climb or the Waipura forest climb of today were of the category of the climbs in snowdonia and The Peaks. Thats a kiwi version of a small hill... or not worth mentioning hill... UK's biggest ones!

I eventually reached the final ten miles... big hills behind me... flattish road ahead. And then the wind hit... not a tailwind... that just wouldn't be allowed. Side headwind marred my progress those final miles... just to finish me off. I crawled towards Dargaville and came across a lodging with vacancy sign... no thought involved... negotiated a discount and was shown in to a 'unit' consisting of living room.. bedroom and bathroom. I then proceeded to spread my kit everywhere so must be careful tomorrow morning to retrieve everything!

Food next problem and a huge problem it turned out to be... approx 1km away was a fast food takeaway shop. Hmmm cycle... no way in hell... my arse hurt and needed a break.. walk then. Down a hill... round bends.. round more bends and no sign of takeaway.. not even in the distance. Totally fed up I walked the considerable distance back. Which is why dinner consisted of a can of tuna... some cashew nuts... and 2 plums (from campsite) not to mention the gummy snakes that I had bought as something different to eat on the go!

So why do I do this. Struggle and suffer by choice. For those that don't know me .. it began with a song .. Let the River Run... or it may have been The Wind blows away my words. Regardless of which song it was by The Alarm and most importantly Mike Peters... it began a journey. An interrupted one but one that now shines through in my life. You see Mike Peters is not only the lead singer of The Alarm but writes songs that speak to my soul. Oh and he is battling cancer. And he has more energy and drive than you or I put together.

He started Love Hope Strength Foundation and as I followed the music I found myself following him.. the charity... the way he leads his life .. a total inspiration to us all.. whether we suffer from Cancer or not. More recently another who is made from the same mould as Mike is another daily source of inspiration for me (and many others I might add). It is people like these two men that drive me to live my life to the full... to be a stronger.. better version of myself... to help spread the word to fight cancer back! My pain and suffering , real though it is, is a temporary thing. But in my pain and suffering I hope you read between the lines and understand what drives me. Everyone has it in them. This is just the game I choose to play to try and raise more money and awareness.

So if you are enjoying the blogs from the comfort of your armchair.. please help me in my quest and do as so many of you have already done. Help spread the word.. read about the work that LHS is doing and how you can become part of the family I am in (www.lovehopestrength.co.uk).

If you feel you can .. please donate to my bike ride page www.justgiving.com/GoWithTheCrazy (*For anyone reading this now the journey has finished - a donation can be made to Love Hope Strength via Just giving at* https://www.justgiving.com/lhsf *)*and help keep the smile on my face no matter how bad my day has been!

Like my facebook page and share with others
www.facebook.com/OneChallengeAtATime

Become a bone marrow donor - its not the painful procedure it used to be: www.deletebloodcancer.co.uk (our partner charity for getting people on the bone marrow donor list)

Together we can Fight back against Cancer!
Thank you for being part of my journey.

All the words in the world will not be adequate to explain about Mike, his music and Love Hope Strength and what it all means to me but I hope that you will go and find out for yourselves if you are already not captivated.

Reading again about this day - two things struck me once again. The Kauri tree - goddam it was REALLY big and how glad I am to have seen it. 'Tourist trap' it may be but I can still feel vividly the awe I felt at being in it's presence and the impression of the 'circle of life' that it inspired.

Secondly was the amount of time sorting out kit took up out of my life whilst on the road. If I wasn't packing it, I was unpacking it... By the end of the journey I had got pretty slick at it but at the beginning, it was not an automatic procedure in the mornings and I hadn't worked out the best way to go about it. Polishing the routine of packing, getting everything packed right, with the things I used most in the most accessible places and ensuring that it was all kept in good order, became a source of pride and even competition with myself. In fact, it was a very calming thing to do, when the worries about the road that day, or aches and pains invade in the morning calm. It distracts and provides a routine to set up the day with. Perhaps also a bit of superstition there also - if it's not done right, then this day will not go to plan - crept in there.

Similarly my evenings had a routine to them. Unpacking off bike clothes and wash kit - shower - charge stuff - find food and eat - blog - answer fb messages.

So many things to be done. Every now and again I would fall asleep blogging, the tablet resting on my chest, but for the most part I was up to well gone 1am and up by 6am. And underneath it all - the road calling me to go and share the day with it echoing into my dreams.

Day 7
The Road is a place for dreamers

Once again todays blog title eludes me just now as Im not sure yet where Im going with it.

Its been a strange day.. not all bad... certainly not all good. There have been tears, there's been a lot of sweat, a possible slight descent into madness only to emerge, having survived another day in this beautiful harsh (or should that be beautifully harsh?) reality that I have immersed myself into.

It did not start well and all further happenings are blamed on this... I overslept! Not to the extent that would have had Falcus (my work mother) phoning me up with a 'are you coming to work' kinda overslept.. just a 'oh shit' kinda overslept. You follow? This meant that what has previously taken up to 2 hours to complete, now had to take half an hour if I wanted to leave when I had set my mind on.

Just going back a bit.. you remember I stayed at a very nice unit, complete with three rooms to spread my kit over. Well now I had to unspread it. And it didn't take half an hour either. I wasn't out the door till around half 8. The couple that ran Leslie Lodges in Dargaville came out to see me off and very kindly completely waived the fee. What a lovely way to start todays ride, more kindness from strangers. Gordon (good name that- my grandad's) and Lynne - if you read this - thank you ever so much again. It was very kind of you and put a good note on a bad start to the day.

So I hit the road and immediately had a problem of the cleat variety. Unclipping is not the easy thing it should have been. I had already turned the cleat holding screw for easy release on my right foot, which had not had the desired effect and now my left foot, which had previously been the reliable one was getting stuck. It was ok for the first ten miles or so, because they were flat but I equally didn't want to sit down and try sort it out on the roadside mainly

68

because I was already late and the day was going upside down already. More about cleats later....

As I just said the first ten miles or so was pan flat... great I though, make up time! But New Zealand had other ideas... a strong headwind... all the way, coupled with sticky to superglue type tarmac meant that although I probably averaged 10mph ... just... it was hard work. The sun was already shining fiercely and it wasn't proving to be the easy stretch of the day by any means. The scenery reminded me of Oklahoma... stretches of fields, some with cattle.. the odd farmhouse or industrial unit scattered by the roadside. Nothing much to distract from the energy expenditure happening on my bike.

I eventually reached Ruawai , where the road turned and became more comparable with Missouri.... up... down... up.... down.... you get the picture! My aim was to get to the connection of this road, SH12 with SH1 by around 3pm. I had already decided that because of my late start, Helensville was out of the question as a destination today and instead had set my sites on Wellsford.

2 major ongoing issues were hindering my progress, aside from the terrain and the wind... cleats and an exceptionally sore arse!

I have already explained about the cleat issue, what I did not describe is the sheer terror it can put into you when you are halfway up a steep hill, need to stop, and you cant unclip. Picture wobbling, swearing, yanking your foot in all directions... only to realise you have to pedal again or fall off, the danger being that you are not quite sure which side you will fall... into the road? Or down an embankment? This fear induces pre-emptive unclipping, usually at the bottom of a hill, which slows your momentum down, makes peddling harder, and generally ensures that you most certainly wont get up the hill! That was problem number 1.

Problem 2

An arse/groin area that couldn't find a good position on the saddle. Despite copious amounts of Chammy cream, however I positioned myself on the saddle, it was at best uncomfortable and at worst downright bloody painful. This meant that I was shuffling round on that saddle more than ten times the average of Alberto Contador on a time trial bike! Worse somehow (something to do with returning blood flow) was when I lifted my arse off the saddle.. often prompting a small yelp of pain, followed by a loud swear word (different every time).

Combine these two problems and the result halfway up one particularly nasty climb were a few tears of absolute frustration. Quickly dried up as didn't help the situation in the slightest and I was going to have to put up with it until I had got to where I was planning to be.

The rest of the miles to SH1 proceeded with very little notice being taken of the scenery. Concentration on the road, my bike, the pain all kept me very much within my own world of hurt. But even as that was occupying me, the miles were slowly inexorably counting down.

I stopped for a very short break/food/drink just before SH1 as didn't think there were many places to stop and not sure when would arrive at destination. There was a shop called dreams... and on the roof was a giant pair of legs sticking upside down - I took it to mean something for me.. not sure what exactly... but something and chuckled..one of few today.

SH1 and.... cars!! Lots of them. But a wide shoulder to compensate and climbs that were manageable in one attempt due to their slightly decreased gradient and the downhill... oh what wonderful downhill. Longish, sweeping downhill made faster by the drag of passing cars.. so much so I clocked nearly 40mph at one point! It wasn't without its slight danger points, occasional points where the shoulder disappeared but on the whole the cars were respectful of me. All this frenetic activity prompted a somewhat more maniacal chuckle... but a chuckle nonetheless.

I eventually counted down the last mile into Wellsford to find myself at the bottom of another hill. Determined not to find lodging for the night until I'd climbed it, I did so and found myself on the high street and straight into some budget backpacker accommodation.

As I showered off the dirt from the road... it became apparent a) how bruised and battered I was (some of the dirt was bruises) and b) that the mosquitos from the campsite the other night had had breakfast .. lunch and dinner... on me! Literally bitten all over and now aware of it so they started to itch too.

So thats another day done... another set of pedal strokes Closer to home.

The Road is a place for dreamers... my dreams are still alive for another day.

LHS

WARNING: TOO MUCH INFORMATION MAY BE GIVEN OUT BELOW. For those of a sensitive disposition - feel free to skip the next paragraph!

On both this trip and Route 66, my arse, or specifically my saddle sore arse became a topic of conversation. And yes it is funny, hilarious even, when it's not your arse. I can find it funny now, when I think of myself shuffling on the seat to find a less painful position or when I try to explain to non-cyclists the benefits/necessity of chammy cream. A chest infection didn't stop me cycling but saddle sores certainly had that power. In fact just before I sat down to write this bit, one of the professional cyclists taking part in the Giro d'Italia (a three week cycle race through Italy) was forced to pull out because of saddle sores. It is an embarrassing topic amongst non-cyclists and sometimes even skirted by those who cycle but it is a very real problem. For me- I seem to have one really bad day where my arse doesn't want to touch the saddle - I remember clearly a similar day out on Route 66 - but then it kicks me into gear to apply cream regularly and air out the affected areas. This year I went commando in the evenings and smeared all kinds of cream remedies on the affected areas. It seemed to do the trick and I do not remember another day where I suffered like this day from that problem.

The cleats sticking was again another problem I had encountered before and stupidly I did not act straight away and change the cleats as I should have done. I should also have put on a fresh pair of cleats before I left the UK but apparently I need to be taught this lesson twice before I take note. So prior to the next ride (if I end up using cleats), I will ensure a fresh pair - before I set out..

Riding on busy roads has never really been a problem for me. Lately I tell myself that I survived Highway 100 and the Mojave Pass in the USA, so nothing could be as bad as either of those. In fact after struggling along and up narrow roads, it is often a relief to hit a wide road, where the traffic pulls you along... not to mention the slight adrenaline rush that comes with speed and dangerous objects (cars and lorries) nearby.

Day 8
In the beauty of my surroundings

Yesterday due to getting up late and other practical issues , I ended the day in Wellsford... somewhat short of my intended destination of Helensville. Today was going to be different. I had resolve and organisation, in short I was raring to go. Just as I went to add some air into my tyres however, I noticed that my pump had essentially disintegrated and was now totally useless. Bit of a problem if I had a flat. I knew there were bike shops in Auckland but given how the previous days have gone.. I probably wouldn't find it or make it there in time before closing...so I texted a friend (Mark H to the rescue again) as he had said if I needed anything today he could help.

I had managed to find time to look at my cleats closely. The right cleat which was new since a couple days into the ride was slightly misaligned and I adjusted that and then made sure to tighten it up well. The other cleat was old and I set about replacing that one. Then as per Mark Davies' suggestion I squirted a little oil in the pedal. Then everything sorted before half seven, I set off, testing first one cleat then the other, then both again. Seemed to be working very smoothly so set off with a little more confidence.

Now I knew that the first part of the day to Helensville was going to be murder... I even thought I had mentally prepared for it. I was behind schedule by about ... miles and in my head , if I could get to Helensville by lunchtime.., things might be ok.

The first hill was bad... the second had me walking... the third required a ten minute stop, leaning over my handlebars, unable to stop coughing. The downhill sections in between were nice but so short lived and the tarmac was again of treacle variety. I was in despair mode again... I wont tell you how many fantasies I had of someone stopping and offering a lift to Auckland. In fact that passed a great deal of my time... wondering at which point I would down tools and go 'enough!'

The scenery on this section got better and better, mainly because I was climbing up and up. Eventually I reached 'scenic' viewpoint and boy what a view. Stretching out in the sunshine was an array of hills and lakes, with the bright blue sky stretching out above. It was such a stunning view that it snapped me out of the painful rotating headspace that I had become immersed in. Well briefly anyway. I talked to myself... 'you knew this was the worst bit of the day... gets easier after Helensville' ... but it would be so easy to just stop... you are never going to make it to Bluff... more tears.. at the thought of letting everyone down, then renewed determination, then despair. All going up and down in my head in a similar pattern to the hills I was riding up... a never ending cycle and possibly self-perpetuating madness!

I kept reminding myself that I had started early and that this was the worst bit of the day and that if I just kept turning the pedals.. I would get there. I didn't think of the rest of the day... just getting to Helensville.

Once again just as feeling at a low ebb two things cheered me up... firstly a text reminding me why I'm out here... secondly as I stopped (on a hill) I looked to my left and saw two beautiful racehorses and a foal... the scene was just so peaceful that it took the stress right out of me... just by gazing at them for a few minutes.

I pushed on and despite everything in my head I managed to get to Helensville and stopped for much needed food as bonking badly.

I knew that the road from here to Fred Taylor Drive (FTD), my road into the South of Auckland was less hilly and this was part 2 of the day. Mark had texted me to meet up on this road with a pump for me and so I kicked on. Lots of flat with a few hills ... and the inevitable headwind... it wasn't bad going. Soon I saw car headlights flashing and as at the bottom of a hill... I pointed to the top... if I had stopped at the bottom that would have been it for me. I struggled up the hill to find Mark waiting for me. It was so nice to see a friendly face...

.. I would have given him a hug but my greeting was me bent double over my handlebars coughing and spluttering... plus my clothes are really starting to smell so that wouldn't have been fair.

Eventually I recovered enough to thank him for the pump.. and watched him as he disappeared over the horizon... right .. here we go again

The hills from here to FTD were all manageable and pretty soon I found the turn off. And into civilisation I went. It was a good thing I was doing this now as all the traffic was coming out of Auckland so I was going the right way. The roads were good... tarmac was the best I'd had yet ... and although there were hills a plenty... suddenly my legs felt stronger...

I powered through South Auckland.. with plenty to distract me.. managed to avoid stopping in the first motel I saw by sheer force of will... and headed across the bottom of the city through mainly industrial areas. It seemed I picked a bit of a grimy part of the city to go through and it seemed pretty run down.

As I got to the other side of the city.. I began to wonder about where to stay tonight. It was getting late... despite the legs feeling ok as I pottered through the city I was now totally weary and just wanted to stop... but where?

I hadn't seen a single motel sign since that first one and was becoming more and more perplexed with the situation. I asked a few people but they weren't sure either...

Then I saw a vacancy sign and swerved in... only to find that it was a care home facility!!!! They were very nice and did offer me a bed for the night... which I was almost tempted as it would have been funny... but at $135 .. slightly more than I wanted to pay. So continued on until I was pointed to a backpackers type place.

I went in and they found me a room after much debate... shared bathroom facilities and windowless but a bed for the night.

I regret stopping here in a way and not pushing on for a motel as I haven't found the shared shower room and I had to carry my bike up the stairs but was so exhausted I don't think I could have gone one step further.

So tired.. and fell asleep before I finished this blog... hence delayed posting till this morning....

So I emerged triumphant yesterday but feel the need to say that there a still a lot of days to go and I am at the limit of what my body can take... I have already used up a rest day and each day has been a huge effort to keep going. I cant tell you how hard this place is to cycle in and I cant remember Route 66 being this tough... though maybe time has fogged the memory somewhat. I say all this because my greatest fear out here is letting down everyone who believes in me and wanted to alert everyone to the very real possibility that I may not be able to cycle all the way in the time I have set myself...

I WIll however...
Try my hardest every day and strive to take as much pain and suffering as humanly possible to get there...

I will Not give up trying...

Right... time to pack up for another day on the road.
LHS to you all and thank you for the support.
It was the only thing that kept me going yesterday. X

I hadn't thought I would reach Auckland and now I was there it was clear that I didn't think I would be able to get to Bluff. Funnily i don't remember that feeling much... I remember suddenly feeling good as I powered up the smaller hills in Auckland, the legs suddenly switching on and deciding that they were going to play ball.

Speaking of my legs - at times they felt like separate from me - another being apart from me, with their own mind, own stubbornness and weaknesses. So much of how I felt depended on how my legs felt that day.

Ironically - this was the bit I was worried about navigating and it was extremely easy. This was one of the days that I had 'google earthed' my way through and it was a bit weird coming up to intersections and recognising them from what I had seen on my computer... the wonders or perhaps the sadness of modern technology on display!

Day 9
Its about the journey and the stories we live to tell

Started off well... out of the weird crappy accommodation in good time and nose to the wind... leaving behind Auckland with every pedal stroke. Of course no sooner had I gone a mile or so.. a motel had appeared followed by several more. Bloody typical. When you want one.. you cant find one for love or money... now I don't need one they were popping up all over the place.

The aim for today was Matamata... a reasonably ambitious aim given it was around 100 miles away... but had good info that the route towards the end was pretty flat... although maybe marred by the dreaded headwinds that accompany flatness. I had also got off to a good start out of the city as there was good smooth tarmac.
Always bearing in mind the importance of food I stopped off after a hours cycling for breakfast of fruit and pancakes... delicious and deffo the best breakfast so far.

It was all going well... traffic reasonable... hills but not bad ones and a general determination to get the miles done today. I passed through little towns on The Great Road South out of Auckland... ticking them off. My first waypoint was the turning off onto SH2... then South on the SH27 all the way to Matamata. I expected hills for the first 60 miles but after that a pretty pan flat run in.

Obviously as I was in the city still... the scenery was non-existent. I have noticed how like American cities NZ ones are... with avenues of shops .. all one story high.. no people walking around town really either.

I reached Drury... the place I had been aiming for yesterday but hadn't quite made. I rolled into a roundabout to go straight on... out of the corner of my eye and somewhat in slow motion a car came from my left and just kinda drove into me... I had started to put the brakes on as had she (though I bloody had right of way... I had already been on the roundabout) ... and ended up half over the bonnet of her car. I put my hands out to try and protect myself from hitting the car too hard and I was still clipped in. .. once everything had stopped moving... i pulled myself up from the bonnet of the car... unclipped my feet and looked at the driver. Elderly-ish lady... looked back at me...think she mouthed 'are you ok' before driving off. I made my way to the side of the road... stood astride my bike... now visibly shaking. Helmet came off... and then the tears of shock. Through the tears two gentlemen walked up to me... helped me off my bike... led me to their shop.. The Bee Hive .. got a chair for me to sit on and told me they'd seen the whole thing and that I'd done nothing wrong (no weird roundabout laws I didn't know of). Anyway massive thanks to Greg and Andrew for picking me up .. checking my bike and making me smile after that. You guys are stars!!

So that had put a bit of a dent in the day. It did make me more determined and i headed to SH2 with determination. Did I mention it was ridiculously hot and all 25 miles of SH2 were coverless. I had been careful to cover my arms which meant I was even more ridiculously hot. I was getting through litres of the stuff. SH2 was not flat either and in order to get to it I had to take a road called Razorback... for obvious reasons. It was basically a very hot and hilly few miles and the tarmac was no longer the smooth city tarmac... we had gone back to treacle.

It certainly was an effort but made it to the SH27 turn off with a reasonable amount of time in the day left to do the last 45 miles. The promised flats didn't come for what seemed like an age and there was a climb that resembled snake pass in the Peaks for type of climb. .. but New Zealand generally rewards uphill effort well and sweeping round the bends was fun... especially given the view I had ahead of me. Flat fields with the road straight down the valley. To my left mountains in the distance... perhaps reminding me of what awaits me should I manage to get there. They were whispering my name... I could feel it. The scenery distracted well enough for thirty miles. Then I hit a wall. Despite being on the flat mainly a slight headwind had kicked up... just to slow the progress. I think the adrenaline from the morning had also worn off leaving me worn out and crawling along. .. so once again I phoned a friend (not Mark this time), the niece of a work colleague. Rachel (hope spelt right) had offered to rescue if stuck and offered a bed for the night. I asked for both and then sat in a layby awaiting a pick up.

Whilst I sat there I had a bit of an epiphany... yes this ride was meant to challenge me and push me to my limits but even more ... it is all about the journey and the stories I live to tell. And whilst Im not totally happy with the decision... it meant that I could be somewhere warm and safe. Also.. the wrist of the hand I had used to brace the impact of hotting the bonnet was starting to hurt slightly. All in all I want to get to Bluff and experience a journey along the way so I have decided in the grand scheme of things that pick up and drive to accommodation was the right thing to do after todays happening. Rachael and Chad were very accommodating in their embracing of the randomness... accepting a complete stranger into their home... cooking me a wonderful dinner and making me feel very welcome. Rescued me in every sense of the word... and my words cannot describe the appreciation I have.

Also Rachel works on a Stud Farm and thats where they live so got to satisfy a bit of curiosity and asked lots of questions... there are some similarities between what she does and what I do which made me laugh!!

So as I sit here blogging... it is with satisfaction for the day... I pretty much covered a massive distance over bumpy terrain and then put the metal to the pedal for as long as my body could possibly take... I've met some more lovely people ... and above all I'm alive and living life to the full.

This country is creeping into my skin and the challenge remains met so far... but at the end of the day...

It's about the journey
X

One incident that I left out of this blog and which has just come back to me is that whilst I was waiting for Rachel, a cyclist cycled past the tired dirty bedraggled heap that was me and came back to check I was ok. not sure how many car drivers would have done this. The camaraderie of cyclists crosses boundaries that others fear to cross. Basically if you are a cyclist, and you see another cyclist stopped - firstly you check out their equipment (their bike - you dirty minded lot), then you check they are ok and if they need anything. Same as cyclists all nod to each other on the road - that's if they haven't stopped to chat!

Rachel and Chad were amongst the litany of people that prove that humanity is alive and kicking out in the world - fighting back all the evil and bad things that happen, with a smile, kind word, help to a stranger. Sitting in their kitchen, gazing out at the grazing horses, I reflected on the journey and how these people who were complete strangers were now a part of the story, part of the tale that was being woven and one of the strings that had held my body and soul together and how many events in both our lives had led us to this very point.... I could excuse the strange thoughts with weariness of body and mind but actually I quite liked the thought.

Day 10
Every day I get up off the floor

Every day I get up off the floor
Keep on coming back for more and more
As the road opens up in front of my eyes
The only limitation is in my mind

Headspace well and truly sorted.

Today Was a good day!

It started with the usual routine of checking messages... packing non bike clothes and wash kit away and pulling on my cycling outfit... which thanks to Rachael my cycling shorts were freshly laundered... helping with that all important hygiene issue. Chammy cream application.. must not forget that bit!

Then pack up the electrical kit and rucksack before filling up the water bottles. Everything charged overnight. Phones into pockets.. SPOT on. Then nothing for it but to say goodbye to my safety blanket of Rachael and her family before heading out on the open road.

Something was different this morning... I had plans.. but more of that later. For now it was enough to trundle along enjoying the cooler air with a bit of misty rain as I wound my way round the quiet country lanes to the main road and Rotorua.. my first big waypoint of the day.

I knew there were hills... I didn't worry. I had set out nice and early and had plenty of time to cover the 73 or so miles to my intended campsite on SH5 between Rotorua and Taupo.

After an hour of cycling.. I breakfasted and in no time at all was back on the road. The gradient began to snake inexorably upwards. The hills were long but my legs felt good... as did my mind. Today was the day... push on... keep on schedule... and maybe if time do a bit of the tourist thing. That was my main aim. Push past Rotorua in time to go to Wai-O-Tapu (sacred waters). A spectacular area of geothermal activity. But although yesterday was about the journey.. today was to be a 'keep on schedule' day.

The road ran up and as it did bisected some lovely forest.. the bush encroaching on the road so much that at one point it created a tunnel through which the road passed. Beautiful but quite narrow and after yesterdays incident I felt a little nervous of the traffic. Sections of this road had no shoulder and my back light was blinking furiously to make me more visible.. especially amongst the trees.

Fortunately today was not hot to start with. Drizzle kept me cool as I kept climbing. The legs were good and despite the awful tarmac in places... I made good time up the hill towards Rotorua. The climb was miles in length but good gradient meaning that I didn't stop for long periods of the climb. I reckon there was a good ten miles of up ness. But instead of hating the up... I was actually enjoying it. The sounds of the bush penetrated through the Ipod mixing songs and the sound of nature in what was actually incredibly harmonious. When I did stop.. the cough reared its ugly head

Then came my reward... a long fast sweeping downhill with views of Rotorua lake. Thundering down.. I actually hit a high speed of 67.3mph (according to my Garmin).. Awesome!!!! About two thirds of the way down I noticed some poor sod... with panniers... on his way up. We exchanged greetings as we passed and then as we were shouting across the road.. I skipped over and cycled up to him (cyclists etiquette ... I was going downhill therefore the task of going over was mine).

Tom was a UK lad who had been touring round a lot of NZ and before that Australia. We compared kit notes and routes and advised on each others day to come. Useful info! It was nice to meet another crazy fool... I mean touring cyclist... I hadn't seen many weighed down as I was.. though didn't envy the panniers. Safe onward journey Tom. I look forward to following your adventures on fb!

It was time to go as time was ticking on and I turned and pointed downwards. Rotorua was a typical NZ town .. looks like a US one but the bonus for me was the 'town tarmac'. Smooth ... smooth... I will be dreaming of smooth tarmac when this is done! I was waiting for the sulphur smell to hit me but was rather disappointed as a whiff only came my way once or twice. As I left the city (having had a very nice pie for lunch- steak and cheese before you ask!) I passed signs for a geothermal area .. one of many... and as I glanced into the distance you could clearly see a plume of smoke rising from the trees. I didn't stop at this one because I knew Wai-O-Tapu was closer to my route with only a few Km detour. And once again I found myself climbing... only I'd lost my legs at lunch.

It took a few hills to find them again. On this stretch of road there was a bike specific path that ran alongside the road. Smooth concrete and running through areas of forested shade it seemed ideal. The sun was now burning hot and a bit of shade was very welcome. BUT... as I ran along this path.. I became a bit miffed. I was often climbing where the road was flat or down... thats not fair. The price to pay for smooth path perhaps but it was annoying me. Don't ask why... it just was. So I returned to the road and its jarring treacle tarmac and although my arse was not thanking me... my head was in a much better place.

So about my arse... I have now perfected the two cheek shuffle. A manoeuvre that enables a rider to continue peddling whilst sharing the pain over the two arse cheeks. It means at one time.. more pressure is on the left side... little shuffle whilst peddling and hey presto the pressure shifts to the other cheek... hey whatever works. By no means keeping me pain free but more bearable and without the constant stops... its a more efficient way of covering mileage.

So I had made pretty good time over the hills and out of Rotorua and when I reached Wai-O-Tapu I decided I had time to detour .. despite my other thoughts which I will discuss later.. I really wanted to see this.   The whole area is 18 sq. Km of boiling geothermal activity dating back 160,000 years. I'd read about it... I'd seen pictures... I wanted to stand on the edge of this natural wonder and breathe in the sulphur. So off the main road I went... down.. and down. I was groaning outwardly at the thought of climbing back up and almost turned round but I had come halfway so continued down.. the sulphur smell already permeating the air.

I got to the visitor centre where it initially looked like my plans would be scuppered as they wanted me to leave my bike in the bike rack outside... errr nope. Much pleading and begging later they let me put it round the side and promised to keep an eye on it. The girl at the till whispered that she would have given me a discount but her boss was watching... so I paid up and feeling a bit weird without my bike... ran down the path... determined to see as much as possible in the shortest time possible as I had other fish to fry!

The first place I came to was Devils pool and it was bright green... incandescent even. It looked alien... how can water be that colour. ?

And so beautiful. The rocks around were brightly coloured yellow and orange which stood out in stark contrast to the grey rock on the surface. Steam rose all around... it was very primordial in its nature and feeling. The next stop was the champagne lake and blue smoke rose from this bubbling lake with greens and orange hues all around. As I went round the lake , the wind blew the steam.. now already cooled slightly, through where I walked and the heat was immense... like walking into a sauna. Then came the walkway across the lake... bubbling holes in the rocks on the other side... geysers waiting to explode.

It really was a sight to behold but it was now almost half four and I needed to be on the road again. My planned night stop was around 15 miles away... but as I climbed the hills to here... the heat had distorted my thinking. Could I.... maybe if.... what about.... it could be possible!! Lets go for it. So the metal went down on the pedals as the gradient went down for a bit I was whizzing along... high from having seen the sights.

Onward to my planned campsite... 15 miles... some ups but a bit of down too...

10 miles... 5..... there it is!

I put my head down and sped right past... fully aware there was no more accommodation for at least 15 miles and maybe 20. I had been planning this all day. Tomorrow had looked to be an exceptionally long and tough day with over 8000ft of climbing spread out over approx 95 miles. If ... as I had planned... I could take a little more punishment today.. I would actually be ahead of the curve in this game that I choose to play. I kept going till I was far enough past it that there was no point of return ... then gulped down a biscuit or two and re hydrated. Then back on it. The cycling gods gifted me good tarmac for 5 miles of nice downhill and I sped along... a bit too cockily perhaps because the cycling gods noticed and simultaneously delivered me a headwind... bad tarmac and uphill. The effort expended to go very slowly was enormous and I was beginning to regret my new found confidence... how the mighty fall. I was crawling... metaphorically on my hands and knees... when on my Ipod... with impeccable timing came Without a fight. For those who don't know the song... it goes like this

Try to stop me... I will carry on..
Try to oppose me.. I will prevail.
My life has been shot down
Im not ready to fall

The chorus being...

I'll never give it up WITHOUT A FIGHT

A special song for some of us and it gave me strength to push harder down on the pedals ... endure more pain... keep going... just keep the pedals turning. No room for doubt... no phone a friend... just me verses the road... my little battle for the day. I was still going slowly and the hills kept coming.. but the evening sunshine coupled with the song and the view stretching out over green fields to the volcanic hills and beyond... plumes of geothermal activity visible on the horizon.. meant none of the pain mattered. I would get there come hell or high water... however long it took.

I reached the place I thought there was a motel only to see it boarded up. I had to go further... into Taupo. No matter... I would do what was necessary and the road was not going to win today!

The first place I came to was an upmarket resort and I did hesitate given my state of road travelled.. fcuk em I thought... I've cycled from the Cape. So in I went and cheekily asked for a discount. The chap at reception got his manager who came out and kinda looked me up and down and suggested a cheaper alternative down the road... I said this was fine and she asked me to prove what I was doing as normally people apply by email. Lol. I gave her a card and did my charity spiel ... thinking that it would have been a lot of effort just to get a discount! In the end she offered $30 off the price and suggested I leave my bike in the porters lodge... that was her funniest yet. I graciously refused that offer and went round to my luxury room and immediately jumped in the shower.

The dirt and grime washed off... only I scrubbed hard in one place only to realise it was a massive bruise I wash trying to wash off.
Braving the restaurant in my filthy off bike clothes.. I asked if I was dressed ok as they had a dress code... I explained what I was doing and as a woman walked past she said .. of course its alright and grinned at me.

Dinner was nice... healthy greek salad.. bruchetta and some chips. Just the right amount. As I was almost done a gentleman on the opposite table asked if I was actually doing what it said on my t- shirt so I had a nice chat with him and his friends about the ride before running back to my room to start charging stuff and reading everyone's lovely messages of support.

I have found the previous days tough going as my body wasn't doing what my mind wanted it to do... today I found some strength and in part that came from all of you... you are as much a part of this journey as I am.

Today hurt but I am now around 20 miles ahead of schedule.... wriggle room.

Today I prevailed... these dreams are coming true.

If you are enjoying these blogs and feel you can sponsor me... please go to www.justgiving.com/GoWithTheCrazy *(For anyone reading this now the journey has finished - a donation can be made to Love Hope Strength via Just giving at* https://www.justgiving.com/lhsf *)*

The phoenix is rising... this journey is for the phoenix.

LHS

Another fantastic day - Wai-O-Tapu was a sight to be seen and I'm so glad I made it there. Like the Giant tree further North - it was an example of the longevity and power of nature and breathtaking to behold. The colours and the heat rising from the depths of the earth were startling and made a lasting impression.

What shone through today was a steely determination. Feeling good having caught up on my self-imposed schedule after the difficulties at the beginning felt so good and the temptation to be ahead of schedule was a driving force.

This is the second time I have gone into a 4-5 star hotel dragging my dirty bike and filthy self along - the first time was in America where I was kindly introduced to the manager by friends of friends. He was very welcoming and tried to put me at ease in the luxurious surroundings (Crystal chandeliers anyone?) This place couldn't have given me a greeting more opposite end of the spectrum. But it made me laugh.... the look the receptionist gave me... but it was like water off a duck's back. Very rarely do i feel smug but here I did because she was judging me from my appearance and I knew what I had been through to get me there... the words - take that look and shove it where the sun don't shine' might have formed in my brain - fortunately that's where that thought stayed, otherwise I might not have had such a comfortable night! However at the end of the day, 5*, 4* or backpackers accommodation, it made very little difference to me - they all had a bed and a shower and that's pretty much all I needed or used. Long distance bike rides - the great class leveller!!

Day 11
In the beauty of my surroundings....

.... I completely bonked. But that bit comes later.

Today was a day of two parts... feeling great and feeling awful.

Part 1
It started off well with a quick and organised pack up and check out of the posh hotel and on the road by half seven. The morning was misty and cool but you could tell that the sun was going to kick in with a vengeance as it was already burning the mist away.

The road that I had taken to find accommodation was the one through Taupo. I had been thinking of detouring that way anyway because there was a .. Giant bike. Now Ive seen the worlds largest rocking chair and the largest Route 66 sign... it would be rude not to pass up this opportunity.

It was pretty cool and my bike looked quite pathetic next to it. Painted in polkadot king of the mountains livery... probably only of interest to cycling nuts like me... it was nevertheless an early morning sightsee tick off.

So then rolled down to Taupo for breakfast... smooth town tarmac meant the wheels rolled well. Breakfast bacon buttie and chai latte set me up for what could be a long hard day and I was pretty nervous about it. Even having done the extra mileage yesterday wasn't going to help much in this ambitious plan for the day. Borne out of necessity... there being nowhere to stop between Taupo and Eskdale... 84 miles and over 5600ft of climbing to face... like I said... it was going to be a long day. Add in what was to reach 30 degrees C and it could be a recipe for disaster. But that was to come....

From Taupo there was a steep climb out of the town as seems to be the way and then I was on SH5... the long road to Napier. Very quickly I had gained a huge amount of elevation and was out in the middle of nowhere. The road bisected forestry land and pine trees were all around me... filling the air with their scent.

The road was reasonably smooth tarmac in most places and rolled up and down... nothing big... just enough to stretch the legs... which were feeling ok at this point. I was surprised because yesterday had been a mammoth day of around 94 miles. I loved this bit of the country. After the forest came the endless grazing meadows... with the mountains in the distance.. the sky a brilliant blue with wisps of white cloud floating gently through the sky. An idyllic place. I then decided to put plan 1 into action for the day.

As my cough is gradually getting better I can almost sing whilst cycling and given the road was ok.. thought it was time to record a video of me singing 'It's alright... It's ok' as I had shaken David Johnston's hand in an agreement to do with this... as we speak I'm trying to upload it but not sure of the sound quality and the internet connection here with my TEP device is a bit slow.. so they may have escaped... for now! It did however make me smile trying to record it.

I pottered along at a reasonable pace and the thought crossed my mind that today was going bloody well. No sooner had I thought it.. did I curse myself as there is nothing better that the cycling gods like to do more than laugh at a cocky cyclist! But more of that later.

Did I mention it was hot. This part of the road took me until 11:30 to cover and I had already emptied one water bottle. I knew of a couple of cafes along the route to refill but it still had me concerned.

At around 11:30.. I pulled into the first of these... the next was a long way down the road.. so decided to have an early lunch. I ordered a couple of spring rolls and a can of fanta and went outside to sit on my still very sore arse. Whilst I was there I got chatting to a lovely Swedish couple about the charity and the ride ... Pia and Mats had been touring around in a camper but were due to go back home soon. I gave them my One Challenge At A Time card and told them about the blogs. Pia wanted a photo of me and my cycling top with the LHS logo. I did enjoy chatting to them. They asked how they could sponsor me and I directed them towards my www.justgiving.com/GoWithTheCrazy and then Mats presented me with a rather large NZ$ bill. Such kindness from strangers yet again. Completely restores faith in humanity when you meet people such as this couple. They reminded me of Faith and Tom, who I met at a cafe on Route 66, the same kindness of spirit. As they got up to leave, Mats gave me his card. On it was the quote ' It's not the destination.. It's the journey' I couldn't believe it.. given I had just written a blog post on the same theme. Do you believe in coincidence??

I got one of those hair on the back of my neck moments... weirdly it seemed as if our paths were meant to cross. So Pia and Mats.. if you read this... it was wonderful to meet you. Safe travels home
I hope this journey provided stories and memories for years to come.

As they left.. the waitress ?owner of the cafe came out and donated to the ride.. went back inside and came out with an ice cream for me. I had been double whammied with kindness and generosity and it brought tears to my eyes.

Time to get back on the road.. because although cockily I thought today was a bit of a breeze there were still a few miles to go and I was aware of the fickle cycling gods. As the next ten miles ticked down.. the scenery changed.. no longer pasture but changed into sandy gorges. It reminded me of New Mexico with the colours..

The gradient began to go upwards as I climbed into the mountain range that I was to cross to get to Napier. As the road climbed.. the view got more breathtaking. Mountains covered with green foliage stretching down into the river gorge. The road cut through with high sandbanks on either side and I began to sweat... buckets. So much so insects were landing on me for their daily water uptake. The legs started well and climbed well and the confidence came back Too soon. The hill climb went on and on... reaching ever skywards. The heat was all consuming and my preoccupation with water grew as the levels depleted. The first big climb done.. there was an ample downhill reward but before long I was climbing again.

This climb was a proper mountain road barriered climb. I was worried about trucks and my legs went into overdrive. I had to stop a few times but was careful not to do that on bends.. which the trucks come haring around.. using every inch of the road including the shoulder.. engines screaming to haul their massive loads.

I was lucky on this climb.. no trucks passed me and I stopped at the top to shove some calories in. A couple stopped in a lay-by next to me and the gentleman enquired if id just cycled up... yup... fair play he said. Just then two logging trucks roared up and I was able to get some good pictures of these workhorses. Ironically it has been pointed out that I was standing next to a wooden cross whilst photographing the probable culprit!

Part 2

That climb done... I screamed down the other side... racing so fast and having a whale of a time. It was short lived. F$#@^&g massive climb number 2 appeared. ...

And my legs failed... imploded... became a jellied mass that I could no longer control.

It was hike a bike time. At least I would keep forward and upward momentum. So I walked and then tried to cycle again... no good.

Complete bonk. So I sat on the side of the road and stuffed more food into my mouth.. rationing the water slightly as starting to run low. Still couldn't cycle so walked the rest of the climb reasoning that it took as long as it took. I knew I had some good downhill after this for a bit. The downhill came as promised and restored my legs a little but the cafe I was expecting was shut and I had very little water. Nothing for it but to push on. A bit of flat with some smaller inclines thrown in and it was getting later... would I be crawling out of the mountains after dark??

I came across a couple stopped in their van. I had been staring at the mountain wall looming in front of me... becoming more and more aware that there was yet another test laughing at me. The water was almost gone and the sun was still intense even though it was 1500. I asked the couple if they had a bottle of water I could buy and the lady just gave me the rest of their supplies... half of my bottle. It was something. I headed on up... desperately aware that my legs were at this point of the day not equipped to handle such a climb. I got halfway up... turned and below me... stretched out for miles was a stunning vista of mountains and green bush.

Once again I could go no further... too steep and my legs were not responding to commands. So I hiked a bike again. Resigned to a very late finish and possible darkness. But I walked quickly and got to the top by 17:40. Which left 25 miles of mainly downhill to the coast and my planned campsite in Eskdale. The worst was over. I still needed more water but there was nowhere to resupply so I ploughed on down.

My heart sank every time it saw a 'passing lane' sign as it deemed the hill steep enough to need one. Crawling on I crested another 4 passing lane type hills.. not as bad as the other one.. but energy sapping nonetheless. It took an age... my throat was burning dry and as I finally got to Eskdale.. the sign for the campsite loomed. I knew it was away from the road.. but couldn't even see it .. so decided to continue on another 3-4 miles until I found a motel.

Where I got the strength to keep the pedals turning.. i have no idea but turn they did until I reached Bay view... dived into the bar and got the last cabin. Thank fcuk for that as couldn't have gone any further.

So once again I made it and looking at my schedule .. was planning to stop further back in Te Pohue but hadn't seen any accommodation there anyway. So I'm ahead of schedule with an 'easy' 42 miles to do tomorrow... unless I push on and aim for Dannevirke which is tempting - another 80+ mile day.

Today hurt... a shiteload in fact and there were times when I thought I wouldn't make it.. but I did.

There was much beauty in my surroundings today but this was eclipsed by the beauty in the kindness of strangers.. making this about the journey once again.

Face Everything And Rise... F.E.A.R

This day looms as one of - if not THE - toughest day I experienced. The heat coupled with the extreme amount of climbing. And yet I did not break... amazingly so.. mostly so to me. It gave me confidence that I could face whatever this wild country threw at me - that belief never really held totally firm but this is where I started to believe that I might make it.

The coincidence of Mats card and the saying on it still resounds greatly - what are the chances?

The thought of running out of water scared me somewhat - it was the only point on the journey that I felt any fear... needlessly so most likely as I'm certain I wouldn't have died from dehydration in the last 30 miles but it did make me feel vulnerable. I wasn't miles away from civilisation in actuality but out there at the bottom of that last climb, with the sun beating down, I felt like I was in the middle of the Sahara. This area didn't appear to have any streams and the river was in the valley far below and most definitely inaccessible. It was a good lesson to have about the amount of water I may have to carry on future adventures where it may be just as desolate if not more so. Weirdly as I'm writing this - I just had a message from a friend - Rob Hurst - informing me about a new water bottle that 'makes water out of thin air'. I had heard of them but from what I understand you need a hot humid climate for them to work - but it is something I will bear in mind for future wanderings!!

Day 12
Dream Aloud

Woke up nice and early feeling pretty rested after a solid 5 hours sleep. Had packed up and was on the road early... bout 07:15. In fact everything in Bay View was still shut so I continued on with a plan to get breakfast in Napier. Much had been made of this day being flat and as I cycled down into Napier.. I cautioned myself not to get too excited because flat isn't ever totally flat and flat generally means wind of some kind... usually a headwind.. so this could still be a difficult day.

I was speeding along at around 14-15mph when finally Hawkes Bay actually came into view. Yeah it was nice but soon was rolling through an industrial bit.. hiding the view. I saw a cafe and stopped.. ordered a huge breakfast... couldn't eat it all... and set off again.

Eventually I was rolling along a nice bike/fitness path with a beautiful view of the water. Fluffy clouds being lit up by the early morning sunshine and rays of sun coming through the clouds .. hitting the water just so. It was quiet on the bike path and more importantly... the tarmac was smooth. Napier was clearly stingier than other towns as I got no 'town tarmac' and my arms and hands were being jolted mercilessly.

I had a plan of pushing on to Dannevirk and perhaps making up an entire day in hand... and as I rolled along the flat road down to Hastings... I worked out in my head.. jumping on ferry a day early... having 2 days off at the glacier... plans forming, concocting, fluidity in motion.

The scenery was once again spectacular... once I got out of the cities. Rolling pastures with hills in the background. Cattle grazing silently
The sun started to really beat down fiercely. After yesterdays water disaster .. I was ensuring to drink regularly. Refilling bottles wasn't a problem as along this road were dotted cafes and little villages at regular intervals... but it was energy sapping nonetheless.

Whilst I rode along the flatter landscape, it was easier for the mind to wander. Given the amount of punishment my body had endured.. especially during the days that I wasn't well.. it was surprising to me that I was still on schedule... even more that I was slightly ahead. It is a testament to the wonder of the human body and mind. These thoughts then turned to a challenge that has been preoccupying my mind since this one was planned and ready to go...

A race... 2700 miles.. from Banff in Canada to Antelope wells on the New Mexico border with Mexico. Self supported.. its classed as the hardest race in the world. The Tour Divide had captured and captivated me...

Many try ... many fail to complete it.. but this is one thing where to line up at the start is an achievement. It is saying that I'm not afraid to try... Even if I fail at least I would have given it a go. And thats what life is about. For so many people fear of failure... of looking foolish to others.. stops them from even trying. Fight The Fear and only then can you truly live.

So although since struggling here on some days.. and even if I don't get to Bluff. it will not be because I didn't fight the fear and it wont stop me dreaming aloud.

Speaking of struggling... as the scenery changed and I encountered my first real incline of the day... it became apparent that my legs were not in the game today.

They did this weird thing where after a stop, no matter what length, the first 30 seconds of cycling again consisted of such an ache in the legs, it was almost painful. I had to grit my teeth and push through it because after 30 seconds it became ok again. Very strange. But I had to stop frequently as I had no power in the legs on any kind of incline and was going very slowly. The wind had picked up a little adding extra resistance and my head started to rearrange the plans for the day. Between where I was and Dannevirke there was at least one reasonable climb to over 1000ft. Nothing compared with yesterday... but given the state of my legs .. it might well feel like it.

Another option... plan d.. crept into my head. It was only 20 miles to Waipukuru.. the place that I was scheduled to stop at today. This would mean a 'short' day of 60 miles but as I had already done over 40 and it wasn't even lunchtime, I figured I could get there early enough to have a decent rest for the legs.. rest and take extra care of my now very sore arse and eat and drink a small fortune. It seemed like a sensible plan within the 'crazy'. Even as I had decided that that was what I was going to do... my head argued with itself... it was still early... after the climb it was downhill to Dannevirke... There was only another 25 ish miles to get there...

All these thoughts were reasonable and well argued in my head. Counter arguments were thrown back... yes but you will have done 60miles.. thats not taking it easy... there is no benefit to trying to gain an extra day if it kills the legs for the South Island... I have to be at Franz Joseph on a certain day as have booked my rest day and a helihike.. i cant just pitch up early....

And so it went on... well until the next incline... that decided it. Waipukuru it was and it was only 13 miles away. Of course now my head had made a decision ... my legs had totally gone. I went through a really nice village 2 miles from my new destination. It had a lovely clocktower and a museum about the history of the town.. the oldest established in the Hawkes Bay area. Waipawa was sweet and it took a lot of mental strength not to just stop there... but then I would be behind schedule again and that wouldn't have been good for the headspace.

So I struggled for the last two miles and passed one motel with a no vacancy sign and went on to the only other hotel in the town. Crawled into the bar and enquired re a room... we are full! Ahhggggg!! Then 'oh maybe we have a room.. hold on'. 5 mins later ... returned with a key and we got chatting about what I was doing.. another gentleman also approached and asked some questions about what I was doing. Everyone else in the crammed bar took turns to stare at me. I possibly looked a bit sweaty.. tired... grimy... road worn!

As I was being shown my room, I thought to ask about cost.. just in case it was $200 or something ridiculous. For you, as you are doing the ride for charity- $50. Perfect.
I settled in my room.. changed... ordered a pizza at the bar... managing to devour most of it in a very short space of time.. then wandered into town in the hope of sorting a pressing issue.

Yup Im going to talk about my arse again (mainly for the benefit of my gorgeous twin cousins.. Danny and Nathan.. who find all this talk of arses hilarious... so much so I've been told it gets their attention away from their Ipads!!) To put it frankly.. the pain was just bearable today. The two cheek shuffle wasn't helping much and I was beginning to get concerned that it would become so severe I couldn't sit on my bike. So action had to be taken in the form of some kind of healing antiseptic cream. But it was Saturday and round here all the shops... including the pharmacy seem to shut at 1pm.

I eventually found an open supermarket and dived down to the medicine section... Bepanthen or a local heal anything gel. After much contemplation (so much thought put into arse cream cant be good) I went for the Bepanthen.. fingers crossed it did what it said on the tin...an antiseptic cream that helps protect damaged skin from infection.

Then back to the hotel to cram in calories... chocolate... cake... and juice... in preparation to rejoin the road tomorrow.

Weirdly I feel I need to justify stopping early to everyone that is rooting for me to complete this challenge so I hope I have explained my reasons clearly. My head is in it for the long game... I need to keep the phoenix soaring until Bluff.. I need to make sure my body can comply.

As for dreaming aloud... I will give some more details of my future plans in further blogs but suffice to say it will once again push the boundaries as this ride is currently doing.

LHS X

> Whenever you find yourself doubting how far you can go, just remember how far you have come. Remember everything you have faced, all the battles you have won, and all the fears you have overcome.
>
> – Unknown

I neglected to mention... or perhaps just avoided it... that Bepanthen is actually billed as a cream for cracked and sore nipples for breastfeeding mothers. It did however do the job for which I bought it for, admirably and aside for the time when there was a bit of a cream mix up, I was very glad to have purchased it.

As for future plans - the dream continues and the wheels are in motion once again.

Day 13
Walk on and be strong

I woke up this morning having had the longest sleep I have had since I got here, a good 6 hours... but was struggling to get going. I awoke feeling a bit homesick and therefore stuck to fb for slightly longer than I should have.

Eventually I packed up and set off ... only to stop 200 yards later for breakfast. My plans, constantly changing, had now gone back to my original original plan and tonight I wanted to be in a little place called Eketahuna. This would be my jumping off spot for my assault to Wellington tomorrow, but more about that in a bit.

The first bit of todays ride was to Dannevirk and was essentially a long drag up before descending into the town itself. It was around 35 miles away and the plan was to be there lunchtime.

The scenery on this stretch of road was of fields in the valley stretching out either side of the road, flanked by 'hills' (there ya go Lorraine!) Cattle were grazing and I still have seen very few sheep. However there were signs for breeding programs and sheep auctions so they must be around somewhere. Despite the drag upwards, the road was good and the tarmac on a reasonable smooth scale. I was moving at a reasonable pace and even the climb when it came was not insurmountable today.

At one point I was trundling along and got hit in the face by a butterfly. Now I haven't mentioned the butterflies yet and that is an oversight. There have been thousands and thousands. In particular today at times it looked like petals blowing all over just because of the sheer number of them. Many were on the tarmac of the shoulder, possibly dying, but it was like an obstacle course trying to avoid them all the time. They looked kinda like cabbage white butterflies and really it was quite a sight to behold.

Before I reached Dannevirk I came across a little place called Norsewood. The strong viking/danish connection began here. The Danes that emigrated here were mainly employed as labourers to clear the forests ready for settlement. Both Norsewood and Dannevirk seem to be very proud of this connection and history and the towns exploit it for tourist purposes. I pushed on past Norsewood eager to get to Dannevirke before lunch to give a good amount of time to eat and then push on for the last 45 ish miles. The climb just before Dannevirk was a small tester for legs that were not working by days end yesterday... I went slowly and stopped halfway up to 'enjoy the view'. As I started to set off again, I almost fell off because my chain had jammed. Fortunately it was easily dealt with, leaving me with some oily fingers but a working bike.

When I finally reached Dannevirk, I immediately liked the town.. it had a bit of an old world feel to it with some older buildings, which I was informed shortly after that many were being torn down as they weren't earthquake proof! I stopped in a cafe for lunch and got chatting to a nice chap about the ride and LHS. I enjoy that part of my journey... connecting with complete strangers out on the road. So thank you Clarke for your interest and message of support for the ride. It was lovely to meet you.

Pancakes for lunch with bananas..... mmmmmmm

Right then, 45 miles to go. Straight flattish road... oh and a headwind of course. Add to that, the sun was now burning hot and I went back to my previous worries about water. I split the 45 miles up in my head to make it seem better, Woodville first at 15 miles, then another small hop to Pa something, then the final 15 miles to Eketahuna, a place which whenever I mentioned today to people, they pulled a face, and told me there was nothing there. As long as it had a bed and a plug point, I'm good!

The road to Woodville was good smooth tarmac and despite the headwind I made it in just over an hour, which was pretty good going. Another food stop and unfortunately also a wee stop. I say unfortunately, because its quite a process as I'm wearing bib shorts, so I pretty much have to strip off my cycling jersey and baselayer to remove the bib short straps. Quite a palaver and not something I wish to be doing more than once a day if possible, especially contorting in a small cubicle.

I was finally back on the road and the next ten miles to the next little town, went by fast, my headspace being more preoccupied with tomorrow and the climb I knew I was going to have to face. Silly possibly really to be worrying about that today but so many people had drawn a sharp intake of breath when I said I was going over the pass, but then I reasoned that it couldn't be as bad as the Taupo-Napier road and even if it was, i'd just go slowly and hike a bike if necessary. Then there was the downhill to look forward to. Just as I was contemplating all this Walk on, be strong came on my Ipod, part of the Mike Peters/Big Country collaboration, and it was impeccable timing because it filled me with belief for today and tomorrow and gave me todays blog title - Result!!

The last 15 miles to Eketahuna were long, slow, hot, dusty and It took a lot of effort to keep the pedals turning. The cows that I passed were all beginning to wander, on their own accord it seems, towards their evening paddocks, one set going through a tunnel under the road, very well thought out. The hills on either side of the valley were beginning to close together, the pinch point being at my climb tomorrow. One way or another, I'd have to get my arse up it.

I crawled into Eketahuna and fortunately there was a room available.

Then this was the evening in order of importance:

Shower... so bloody good!
Plug in phone, Ipod etc
Put photos up from the day
Food
Fb messages, comments etc- try to reply to most/all
Blog
Zzzzzzzz

So another day done
Walk on, Be strong!

Day 14
High on a Hill and a bit of Strength

My usual packing routine saw me leaving Eketahuna at 07:20... far too early for anything in that little town to be open.. even on a Monday morning. So breakfast was going to have to wait 20 ish miles until I got to Masterton, my first aim for the day.

It was an unbelievably beautiful morning.. the sunshine lighting up the fields of gold and framing the 'hills' on either side of the valley. It wasn't hot yet but the sun warmed the bones as I peddled out of town. I kept my Ipod off this morning.. wanting to hear the early morning sounds of the landscape... and I was already feeling bloody good. Words had been written in the sand this morning filling me with Love Hope and Strength and I kept them with me as I pushed onwards.

I musta broke my speed record for this trip so far as I rattled out the miles to Masterton, lost in thought of what the day could bring... Rimutaka 'Hill' looming large on my horizon. Its all I could think about. Fear could even be used to describe what I felt about the test that was awaiting me... made worse because I didn't know exactly what that test would be like.

Called a hill but described with reverence by everyone I have talked to about it... it could be the stuff of legend.. or it could break me.

I had no choice.. I had to go over it.. and yet it was only a part of my 84 ish mile day. But it swamped my mind.. enveloping me with dread!

Masterton appeared quicker than I expected and I was sitting down having ordered pancakes for breakfast by 0900. When in walked two touring cyclists.. and by touring I mean kitchen sink carrying.

Todd and Luciana were from the USA and were going from south to north. We swopped stories of hills and traffic and mileage and was great to talk shop about two wheeled journeys.

But given I was on a more stretched schedule I devoured my pancakes and hit the road again.
Next stop Featherston and the beginning of 'the climb'!
The twenty miles were made tough on what was a relatively flat road by the headwind that had sprung up.. gusting at times and making it difficult to keep up a good pace. The tarmac wasn't of the reasonable sort most the way either so the two combined were making me work much harder than I would normally have to on a stretch of road such as this!

The fields remained a golden hue and the mountains were pinching the road ever closer together as if to say... 'don't forget we are here'!

As if I could!

Got to Featherstone in a reasonable time though the last 5 miles were of the crawler variety... being beaten into submission by the wind. However ... once there I was determined to have a leisurely lunch and rest.. ready for the test to come. Either that or I was procrastinating. Whichever it was.. I took an hour over lunch and whilst I was sitting there got a surprise call from Lorraine. Now Lorraine is a lovely lady who I met for 5 minutes in the Peak District.. chatting about walks in the area and when she heard I was coming here.. she immediately said she would meet me at the end! How lovely is that! Anyway.. the phone call distracted a little and made me smile so thank you Lorraine... I'm almost on the same Island as you!!

At half one I set off and immediately was climbing... then descending .. then climbing as the pass came into view. You know how things are never as bad as you imagine? Well in this case it was worse... the bit of the pass I could see was incredibly high up and I wasn't sure how the road got up there in such a short space... I took a VERY deep breath and commenced the climb. It was very narrow in places with little or no shoulder to ride on. I developed a strategy of hopping from one wider shoulder bit to another... getting round the bends as fast as I could and staying quite far out in the road on bends so cars and trucks saw me early. The gradient was steep but not impossible and my legs almost felt good!

The view .. whenever I stopped for a break.. became grander as I gained altitude and was verging on breathtaking.

Fortunately few lorries were around and I could hear them coming a mile off... so whenever I heard one I pulled over in a safe place and waited for it to thunder past. I got a lot of waves and a few thumbs up from drivers who appreciated the effort of climbing this thing... and it just went on and on and on. Bend after bend.. narrow with crash barriers on the outside.. I was in a world of hurt... but I was getting up it. 1 and 3/4 hours later I crested the rise with a fist pump to myself and tears sprang unbidden to my eyes. By far the highest hill I'd climbed up on a bike and although it hurt.. I stopped frequently and was pretty slow... I had cycled every inch of the way.

I met a couple from Derbyshire: Stuart and Helen.. who kindly took my photo next to the pass monument (Soldiers had marched from the Featherstone training camp over the pass at the beginning of their journey overseas to fight). We got chatting about the ride and the charity and Helen kindly filled up my top tube bag with sweets to keep me going. They waved goodbye and went sweeping down the mountain. If you are reading this Stuart and Helen.. thanks for the sweets.. they got me to Petone. It was lovely meeting you and I wish you a safe onward journey.

Downhill reward right?? Errr nope. The wind had started to really gust up here and given my light bike every now and again I was caught and blown sideways. This meant I went down very slowly and carefully.. brakes on most the way. Even so.. what had taken me nearly 2 hours to get up... took 15 mins to get down. Once at the bottom the hills hadn't gone completely and with that and the strong headwind ..my legs were turning to jelly again.

Im going to jump forward a bit now... speed through Upper and Lower Hutt to Petone. I had already tried a couple motels in Lower Hutt to no avail and so was forced to continue on. Eventually.. slightly desperate went to one of the beachfront motels to be told that they were fully booked as were most motels in Wellington. Explaining my plight... i.e from Eketahuna.. over the hill etc... Lynnie took pity on me and phoned round a few other motels ... all booked up. Then she said she'd be back and disappeared for a few minutes. On her return she offered me a room in their private living part of the motel for 100$. How kind to open up their own space. As I went in and Lynnie showed me the room she said her husband Graeme had brain tumours which had spread and he was due an operation in two days time to help with the symptoms of his terminal cancer. I then said that I was riding for a cancer charity and explained about LHS. 'Its meant to be then' said Lynnie. Once I'd settled in my room and showered and changed I started to go out for food. Lynnie came over and gave me the $100 back as a donation to the ride. I was so moved by this gesture I couldn't stop thinking all the way to the chinese and back. I wanted to give them something.. both as a thank you and as a gesture of solidarity in Graeme's fight. I looked at my bands.... Love... Hope... Strength...

They mean a lot to me and at the same time I was arguing with myself.. it is only a band.. you have another at home... but will it jinx the journey if I give one away (I couldn't bear to part with them all) . As I went back to the motel.. I was still arguing with myself. I went in and Graeme.. Lynnie and their son Nathan were eating dinner. I took off my strength band and offered it to Graeme as a gesture for his fight ahead. STRENGTH... I wanted to keep love and hope with me but I get my STRENGTH out on the road from all my family and friends supporting me.. it was only a gesture but I tried to convey to Graeme and Lynnie what the bands and the words mean to me.

Tears sprung up in all our eyes... Im so glad I found it in myself to give the band away... only a gesture but the meaning behind it was solidarity in the fight they had ahead.

So today.. the writing was in the sand and I stood victoriously High on the hill... which didn't matter in the end quite as much as giving away some STRENGTH.

I still think a lot about Lynnie and Graeme... how our paths came to cross.. how much I fought with myself about giving away a piece of rubber... how much it meant to me that maybe they understood a small part of what I was trying to say.

I started off by saying words had been written in the sand and they had by my phoenix - words of defiance and full of fight. We all write words in the sand from time to time but how many of us live by those words when it is often easier to compromise or give up. I felt like I had a chance of making the phoenix proud by writing my words in the sand at the top of Rimutuka Hill - writing with all the strength I had left in me by getting to the top.

But sometimes it doesn't matter that we write the words - sometimes all the fight in the world isn't enough. But it does matter that the spirit that wrote the words lives on in everyone else and that is in part what I was trying to do with this journey

Honour the words written in sand - Honour the spirit of the phoenix.

LHS

Day 15
One Step Closer To Home

Wooohoooooo .....

Clean cycling clothes!!! Oh no thats the end of the day ... start again....

My day began what seems an awful lot of hours ago.. last night I had booked the 9am ferry from Wellington to cross to Picton on the south island. Check in was at 08:15 and I had a 6 mile cycle to get to the terminal. 6 miles of unknown track... ?headwind... ? difficult navigation. My point being that I couldn't be late.

So my alarm was set even earlier 04:45 to give me enough time to pack... fb... and get out of the door by 06:45. I tried to creep around so as not to wake Graeme and Lynnie and managed to accomplish everything by half six. As I wheeled my bike out Lynnie was in the kitchen... gave me a hug and wished me well for the journey. I was sad to go because they have been a huge part of what makes this a journey.. despite the fact we only met for a few hours they will live on long in my memories associated with this ride.

As soon as I went out of the motel... the beach was directly in front of me. The day was slightly overcast with spots of rain.. but that didn't detract from the sunrise coming up over the ocean...

revealing the splendour fraction by fraction. No sooner had I started out.. had I stopped to take this photo....

I loved the way the clouds reflected the light and although the pic in no way does it justice... I hope you get the idea. I started on the road but the traffic, as Lynnie had predicted, was wall to wall.. so I dodged onto the cycle track... merrily passing cars till I got to the main road into the city... I travelled on the shoulder, clipping along before being directed back onto a bike path that ran alongside the railway... smooth... no traffic... perfect and the six miles thundered by. I was so fast it might seem that I was racing to get away from the North... but it wasn't that. The North has provided some epic challenges... days that I will never forget... and people, whose deeds of kindness towards a crazy stranger (yup.. thats me.. just in case you were in any doubt) will form part of my stories for years to come. So no, i wasn't racing to get away from the North.. rather forging ahead to see what the South would bring. Genuinely surprised to actually be at the point of boarding the ferry, it did feel like a huge waypoint in the journey and I have to keep reminding myself that Im not done yet... harder days may await me. And yet I guess, much as I love being out here... breathing the air... I also am racing towards home... the familiar... my family and friends... without whom I would not have got this far. The ferry ride symbolises that 'One Step Closer to Home'. Not surprising then that I have felt a little emotional today.. amongst other feelings of amazement that I'm here!

I got to the turnoff for the ferry and immediately directed by signs over a pedestrian bridge and round to the terminal. As walking over the bridge I caught up with Bo Zhang... a cyclist from Shanghai who had ridden from Auckland on a slightly different route to me. He was on a mountain bike with just a rucksack, albeit a large one. We swopped road stories in the walk to the terminal and basic chatter... checked in and got directed to wait outside the terminal building. More chatter and then from Bo...

'Can I ask a question.. I don't mean to offend'... bloody hell what was he going to ask!!!

'Does your arse hurt a lot at the end of the day??'

That made me chuckle... not 5 minutes together as strangers and already discussing 'the arse'. Only in the cycling world. So we discussed chammy cream and healing cream and the need to 'go commando' with cycling shorts.. all in the space of time we were waiting to board!! Bo was good company and of the same philosophy... he was wearing a t shirt.. made himself... with the words.. 'The longest journey starts with a single step' .. words I have written on my bike courtesy of David J I believe!

Eventually we got called to board and rolled the bikes onto the lower car deck where we left them in a bicycle rack and joined the masses in the rush for breakfast!

Then it was up on deck to wave goodbye to the North. Blustery... drizzly but with the sun poking through and the long white cloud visible over the mountains ... it was a fitting picture of the North Island and I turned my back on it and faced forward to the next step of this journey.

There was time to relax in between the north island and entering Marlborough Sound and I did a reasonable impression of someone who has cycled a lot of miles ... chai latte in hand.. in a comfy chair...

Then back up on deck to watch the passage through the sounds.. still grey and overcast and a wind so strong you expected a 'man overboard' shout any moment.. it was still nonetheless spectacular. Little houses were dotted on the shoreline... access by boat only and it was possible to imagine myself getting lost amongst the beaches and hills in this part of the world... so idyllic did it appear.

It was a fairly stunning place and it was through here we were guided into Picton.. there we scrambled to disembark and wheeled our bikes off the ferry.

Then as both me and Bo were heading in same direction we kinda set off together but it was weird as conscious that he was on a slower bike.. I strolled along .. still pulling away.. I stopped to take a photo and he said go on as you are faster.. so I went on... only to be overtaken when I stopped for another photo. He then stopped to retrieve something out of his backpack and waved me onwards... that was the last I saw of him as we then went our separate ways but in that short stretch it served to remind me why I ride alone. It was nice to have a bit of company on the ferry and swop stories but then I think both of us felt a bit awkward as we are used to being solo.

Bo.. it was nice to meet you. Sorry didn't get to say cheerio properly but I hope you enjoy the rest of your ride and that your sore arse recovers!.

The landscape this side already seemed different with the fields less burnt golden and more green. There seemed to be more trees here too and the road ran along the base of the hills... which were covered in greenery.

Once over the incline out of Picton it was mainly downhill or flat... god bless the southerners who didn't see a need to build the road over the hills.. instead winding it round the base of them. I liked my introduction to the South!!

In no time at all I reached my turnoff and Spring Creek campsite.. where I had planned to spend my DAY OFF!! Yup my first proper day off!!! I rolled in and enquired about a cabin. A lodge room was available for 25$ a night (bargain) and in no time at all I was also in the possession of a bag of washing powder.(most important bit.) Then came the kicker... you can lock your bike up outside!... Errr actually I'd like to take it in my room. 'No you cant do that.. it would be like taking your car inside' Nooooooo ... it would be like leaving your child outside!!!

I begged and pleaded... mentioned how clean my bike was and in the end she asked me to wait and she would check. It was a long few minutes but she came back and said it would be ok... great cos if it wasn't I would be taking my beloved bike elsewhere!!

All sorted I then had some priorities... shower to clean myself and laundry to make my cycling kit clean and presentable once again. Which leads me back to the start of this blog...

Wooohooooo clean cycling kit!!
And so I have a scheduled Day off tomorrow... lie in ... and then the day is mine.!

So the North has been left behind and focus turns...

To the south ... to the south..
 My time is running out (ten points to anyone who gets where those lyrics from)

Today was an easy day but one full of significance because I have willed my body to places it didn't want to go and have persevered and am on schedule...

One Step Closer To Home!

LHS ... Day 15 done

i can't tell you how wonderful and indeed exciting to be boarding that ferry... I was what felt like 'half way' through my journey. Complete nonsense in terms of mileage but in a geographical sense anyway. I felt at the time that it was a huge shame that the weather wasn't better for the journey through the straights as it is supposed to be one of the most stunning ferry rides in the world - I saw a lot of cloud, felt very cold and got blown around the deck. Nonetheless maybe it was good that the weather drove into the cabin areas as it meant I had to relax a bit- recharge the batteries a bit, and spoil myself with inactivity for a while.

Cycling along with another human being was nice - for the first 5 minutes then all the reasons why I like solo cycling began to surface. I was faster - less loaded down and faster bike - which made me worry that I was going to fast... if the cleats had been on the other foot then I would have been worried about holding him up. If you cycle with someone else - the complete freedom is gone... then you have to compromise... stop earlier than you would like, eat when you are not hungry etc. Plenty of people manage it however so it must be something in me that recoils at the thought of being tied to another person when out on the road. Part of the reason I cycle is the complete freedom as well as the knowledge that you have to be totally reliant on yourself. People, when with others often fall into a category of leader or follower. Both curb freedom. If you are the one that people are looking to then there is pressure to make all the decisions and try to keep everyone happy (usually at the expense of yourself). If you are the follower, then you lose all your self-reliance, faced with the ignominy of being led along a path (that you or may not want to be led down) It is a delicate balance and one, that I confess, I would be pretty shit at!

Day 16
Rain in the Summertime

Rest day... what the hell do I do with myself? My 'lie in' this morning saw me awake at 0700 and already at a bit of a loss. My usual morning routine of fb... then packing up ready for the day wasn't necessary this morning and it felt a bit weird.

Outside was cold (by my recent standards) and drizzly. It was a very grey morning but I was a bit igity so after an hour or so of catching up with messages I decided to wander by foot into Spring Creek town. From the campsite it is a nice stroll with the river on my left and the road to my right. Past a little nature reserve bit and in a short distance I reached the junction. One small supermarket and a hotel stood here but I wanted breakfast so thought I'd go further into Spring Creek.

The backpackers place was on the left and then it was a single street down... houses to my left and right... past a school and a kindergarten, but no sign of any shops/cafes etc that I have so far found in little towns. Even the ubiquitous Dairy (New Zealand version of a corner shop) wasn't to be found.

Half an hour later ... I ran out of civilisation. The bridge over the river signified the end of Spring Creek. The river looked peaceful and a heron like bird swam across as I stared down.

A couple of photos later and it seemed like there wasn't anything for it but to turn around and find something worthy of breakfast at the shop (4 square). A bit wet now I arrived at the shop again and proceeded to pick out supplies for breakfast and tomorrow. I ended up with rolls and brie for breakfast (mmmmm) and a selection of cereal bars and flapjack type things for tomorrow (more about tomorrow in a bit). I even bought a paper determined to relax into the day. Given the rain I couldn't see myself spending much time outside.... there were plenty more cycling days for me to get wet in!

The brie and rolls went down nicely and I spent a good hour reading the paper. Scientists have worked out how to print larger organs and keep them alive up to and after implantation in animals, George w Bush has been rolled out on the campaign trail to help his brother Jeb and the public buildings were all back open after post earthquake inspections in Christchurch!!

Then I had to do some work!! No rest for the wicked! My poor bike had been crashed into... dealt with rain and gear crunching uphills and now needed a bit of tlc.

But how could I clean the chain properly? I hadn't bought any degreaser with me as the can I had at home was too large. Hindsight a wonderful thing... I should have brought a little in a small container... but thats hindsight for you. Could I just use water ... I didn't think that would work... so I fb messaged a friend... another biking nut... Chris Summerill. (Well done on the bunny hops Chris). A reply quickly came back... WD40... white spirit... or petrol. Could I obtain any of those? I wandered over to the camp reception and asked the random question... ' we have some petrol' came the reply... not a raised eyebrow in sight.... 'bring your bike round the back! So I duly did that and he poured some petrol on a cloth (which I did bring) leaving me to scrub my chain and cogs till they were nice and clean. The oil had now transferred itself to my fingers leaving my hands with oily petrol stains all over... but my chain was clean!!

A further scrubbing got me a bit cleaner and I wheeled my bike back into my room having also rubbed off some of the road grime of the past 15 days.. not quite new again... my bike looked better and I was satisfied that we were prepared for the coming days.

I sat in my room eating chocolate... crisps and sweets... no need for calorie worries as my belt needs to be pulled a little tighter every day. I was just chilling out when there was a knock at my door.....

I opened the door expecting the management or the cleaner outside but there stood this gentleman who quickly introduced himself as Nick... said he'd been following my bike ride, knew The

Alarm and Mike and Jules .. saw I was staying here... and came to see if I was alright or needed anything! What a wonderful surprise!! We chatted for a while and then arranged to have dinner later. So nice to meet someone from home, familiar with the Alarm world and what a lovely gesture to track me down!

When Nick left I spent the afternoon dozing or reading. I also had a mooch at tomorrows 'stage'. I had been made aware of the weather forecast by Andy from Auden guitars who made me aware of some landslips and possible road closures... none of which should affect my route tomorrow. The forecast is for rain and more rain and tomorrow is a long one with very little in between beginning and end points. Running down on SH63 from Spring Creek to Murchison, the road is a long drag up to a point.. then a bit of a climb before the 40 mile gradual descent into Murchison. A total of just over 100 miles.. the first point where there looks like there is anything is St Arnaud at around 60 miles. Which will be fine even in rain as long as there isn't a bad headwind. A bad headwind could destroy my day and make my destination of Murchison a step too far... we will see. I have an option to stop in st Arnaud and make the next day a 100 mile day so will see how it goes... but it could be a late arrival day. And that is tomorrow!

Nick came to pick me up for dinner and I had the luxury of being driven to a nice pub in Blenheim... where to my delight they had pizza!! We spent a nice couple of hours chatting about New Zealand... bike rides... the weather(in true brit style) The Alarm and LHS and all manner of things. It was nice not to be talking out loud to myself for a change... poor Nick had to endure a very chatty Lid. Thank you Nick for tracking me down. It was lovely to meet you.

One of the questions Nick asked me is why I do these rides and it is a good question because often when Im in the middle of them.. I question it myself... what the hell am I doing?? Ive thought about this a lot... what drives me to do this to myself and I have come to these conclusions... some of them may sound cliched but it is what it is....

I find it fascinating to see how much pain and suffering the body can endure when the mind has chosen to do something and asks the body to respond. Both the human body and mind are amazing tools for us to utilise.

YOUR BODY CAN STAND ALMOST ANYTHING, IT'S YOUR MIND YOU HAVE TO CONVINCE.

And the thing is... I'm no athlete... I don't spend hours every day training... I often don't ride properly more than once a week... I struggle like everyone else to motivate myself when its cold.. wet.. and miserable. But despite all that... put me on a bike with a goal to achieve and I will break myself trying to achieve it. And so far I have not broken completely.. partly on occasion... days where the mind is almost ready to give up but something continues to drive me onwards... what is that? Pride possibly.. don't want to be seen as someone who gives up easily... certainly a fear of letting everyone down.. all those people who have invested time in reading the blogs and cheering me on... and then there is the thought that everyday people face much harder challenges than this with quiet endurance and if I can do some good by highlighting that and the cause of LHS then thats a good thing to do.

Then there is the feeling that being on a bike in a strange country with no one to rely on except yourself. It is the best way to see the world.

Lots of people will hire a campervan and drive it from one tourist spot to another... get out... take a photo... and so on. Buy a t shirt at the airport with New Zealand on it and go home happy... and great if that satisfies their needs. But for me... I like to immerse myself in a country. I may not see all the tourist 'hot spots'... I may miss the flat rock or the maori village... but what I get it this:

I have felt every inch of the country that I have peddled through... I have breathed every breath of air and sweated up every inch of the hills... I have absorbed the sounds and the smells of the road and the bush next to it. I have truly lived and absorbed the country in its rawness (and harshness at times) and however far I get I know that I will have truly 'seen' far more of this country than I would have done in a campervan. I meet and can talk to people easier as they are more receptive to someone solo on a bike and I know that in time... the painful and hard bits will become just part of the great story that i get to live and I will be left with a greater sense of achievement than if I'd driven from one end to the other...

Does any of that make sense??

I do believe that anyone is capable of doing something like this... it just requires a small leap of faith beyond the fear and the doubt and the excuses... and then go do it. Its not what everyone would choose to do but it doesn't have to be this... in life... doing something that you fear every once in a while is good for the soul. Life begins at the end of your comfort zone... in that I have every faith!

Few more bits and pieces to do then good kip hopefully and up at 0500 for the routine to begin again. Today I have rested... tomorrow I am on the road.. pushing myself to my limits again.

A massive Thank you to everyone for their support and messages of encouragement. Please keep sharing the blogs and the just giving page (www.justgiving.com/GoWithTheCrazy) so that we can all be part of this journey and raise as much money as possible for LHS.

Fight Back... Be Free .... Stay Alive!

I always have built a couple of rest days into a schedule... you never know when you may need to have an enforced stop and having a couple of days for contingencies always seems like a good idea. SometimesIi use my rest days as a day off the bike but one where I stay active. At other times I have had a little leg stretch but then completely rest. In New Zealand I had 3 rest days built in but in actuality i was forced to use up one of them when I was sick and could only go 30 miles that day, the other one would be the only set in stone day, a sightseeing trip to Franz Joseph glacier, and this was the third one.

Rest days are a bit unpredictable, it feels somewhat wrong to not be packing up in the morning and to call a place 'home' for more than one night. The rhythm of the road has been instilled in me and a rest day disrupts that rhythm. It is also a bit of a gamble that your body will react to the rest day in the right way - and not feel like dragging lead along the next day. In the pro peloton on a three week tour - there are rest days built in, and the next race day is always interesting as one or two riders have generally left their legs behind.

I struggled somewhat with what to fill this day with. It came at a time that wasn't particularly convenient, after a relatively easy day with the ferry ride and was in a place with nothing to do. I put it here in my planning as it seemed to be wise to have a rest day before my assault on the South of the Island and had I put it anywhere else, it would have either been too far away or two close to my immovable rest day at Franz Joseph. The saving grace of this day was that the weather was AWFUL! Torrential downpour most of the day, so at least I avoided being soaked again - not that it made much difference because it seemed that I was destined to be wet and cold most of the rest of this challenge!

The knock on my door and the subsequent meeting with Nick was a huge (welcome) surprise. It still astounds me that he bothered to track me down and search me out. It was also gratifying to know that my little journey had reverberated this far around the world. Thank you Nick for taking the time out of your day to find me - it was lovely to meet you.

I think I explained my reason for this journey in the blog but as yet there is also some indefinable reason - something I cannot quite grasp, something that is within me that drives me. This journey has brought me no closer to an understanding, which might well be a good thing. Maybe I'm not supposed to understand as then the mystery would be gone and with it the drive to experience new things and face new challenges and I don't ever want that. Maybe it's the indefinable that defines me?

Day 17
The wind blew away my words

Apologies for length of blog... a lot to recount today!

Awoke this morning to rain.,. No not just rain, an absolute downpour. It was 0500 and the rain was hammering down. Bugger! No excuses today... just got to go and face it. So packing up took slightly longer as wanted to ensure everything was locked down and watertight. My Apidura bags aren't immune to a deluge but pretty much everything I ned to stay dry is housed within another waterproof bag.. double layering! My off bike shoes were conveniently housed in a plastic bag from my shopping trip the day before, as they are in the webbing on the outside of my rucksack.. all my electrical kit is in another waterproof bag in my rucksack... everything else including me will have to get wet! Rain gear on and poked my head out of the door and to my surprise the rain had pretty much stopped and there were clear skies overhead. The 'hills' had dark clouds hovering above the, but they didn't seem to be moving much.. so I pushed off, eager to make the most of this break in the weather.

Approximately 8 miles down the road I ended in up the small town of Renwick where I did a very small detour to the town centre and found a cafe for breakfast. I was impatient as time was thundering on and I was going to have a long day. The road reports were not great with stories of flooded roads and impassable places although SH63 seemed to be clear. Nonetheless I was impatient to get going. My first aim for the day was St Arnaud.. 66 miles away. I wanted to get there by 2pm, which would give me enough time for the last 35 miles or so to Murchison... that was plan A! There were alternate plans but I told myself to just get to St Arnaud and then see how the land lay.

Breakfast done I set off in the knowledge that there was nothing until I got to St Arnaud. 2 hills stood in my way and for some reason, these held a lot of dread for me. I knew the road up to the climbs was one long steady drag upwards but until the climb it should be reasonably straightforward. Of course I didn't touch any wood when I said that and the cycling gods were paying attention. The sun had started to beat down a bit... not as hot as previous days but enough to make me worry about water supply... nothing until St Arnaud remember.

The road was flanked by hills... and the hills to my right in particular were pretty imposing. Clouds hanging over them and a very jagged appearance whilst being covered in dark green trees. Just next to the road, vineyard after vineyard, organised in neat rows and bringing a semblance of order to this wild landscape. It looked very picturesque in the early morning sun and captivated my attention for a good few miles... until the headwind hit me.

About 10 miles into the day.. the wind sprung up and because I'm a cyclist... inevitably it was a headwind. From trotting along to crawling at around 6 mph it took every ounce of energy to keep moving in a forward direction. My day was going to pot. The one thing I had been truly concerned about was a headwind as because I was heading down a valley on a pretty straight road... once the headwind had sprung up... there was no escaping it. This went on and on.. with no respite whatsoever. I was also going uphill slightly and the 2 combined were sapping me of every grain of energy and motivation I had in me. I was at a very low ebb. Not only were the headwinds destroying me, they were destroying my day and possibly the entire trip from now on, as if I stopped at St Arnaud at only 66 miles, that meant tomorrow would become a 100 mile day and the weather could be even worse rain wise.

My head started focusing on plan B, never good this early in the day.., its like admitting defeat... only there wasn't anything I could do about it. If the headwind continued in this manner I would have to stop at St Arnaud and accept the consequences tomorrow, whatever they may be.

And so it continued. The scenery was becoming more grand as the miles crawled on by and with the sun out, even in the headwind I managed to appreciate how lucky I was to be free in these surroundings. Not a great sign... this showed that I had already given up on my earlier goal of Murchison and was starting to accept plan b.

I cant tell you how much I was aching from battling the wind. Every fibre in my body was screaming at me to stop ... but I knew there was nowhere to stop and I would have to keep plodding along. I did so with an increasingly heavy heart. Add to that because it was warm and I was sweating so much from the effort, my water was already running a bit low, especially when there were two climbs to come.

The first climb was just a slightly steeper extension of the drag up I had been doing all day and was surmounted easily enough. The descent was blighted by the ghastly headwind, so much so that I had to peddle downhill, no free ride today. In the ten miles between that climb and the second one, the road remained reasonably flat and having recalculated time I thought I might get to St Arnauds by 15:00. I knew it was a downhill trend from there to Murchison, but also have discovered that nothing is that simple in this hardland! No counting chickens for certain. It was about 13:00 when I started hallucinating or so I initially though. There in a layby was a campervan, and more incredulously, a food van!! I pulled up to it and touched it to be sure it was real.. it didn't vanish!

On offer were toasties and milkshakes and coffee and bananas and..., and...

130

A lifesaver if you were me and had been battling with every fibre all morning and were worried about running out of water. The lady, from the Philippines originally was serving 3 other customers... all dressed in bee suits. Across the road was their van stacked high with hives. It explained the presence of so many bees in the last few miles and they told me that there were hundreds of hives in this area. They also told me that it had been a bad season for Manuka honey (used for just about everything in these parts) and told me stories of their morning on the road... felled trees... washed out roads. Fortunately none on my route, although I had noticed that the rivers were full to bank bursting proportions and literally thundering along with gallons of dirty water filled with debris. It was quite a sight to behold as previously all the rivers I had crossed had been mere trickles with dry riverbeds. No longer apparently!

Once she had served the beekeepers and they had driven off I ordered a cheese and onion toastie and a vanilla milkshake with a banana as an appetiser. It didn't take long and I sat swatting biting flies off my legs until the lady came and gave me some insect repellant. Pesky things.

It was time to get back in the road, now 13:30 and once again recalculating time and distance in my head (I spend a lot of time doing that). Reaching St Arnaud by 15:00 was still a possibility but in what state?? But things were about to get worse....

15 minutes down the road... a bee flew into my mouth... we both got a shock I'm sure but he hit out first and stung me on the inside of my lower lip.... a few swear words resounded around the previously peaceful countryside... I spat him out and was left with a throbbing pain... enough to distract from the headwind for the next 10 miles. Bees have gone onto my hate list along with dogs!! From that point on, I saw bees everywhere and understandably was a little nervous. I couldn't feel the sting still in my lip but wanted to check so flagged down a passing car and to the bemusement of the two occupants, asked them to check. All good , sting not there ... but now lip was starting to swell a bit and I had a tingling sensation on my right

cheek and jaw. Hence the unhappy lid photo posted... I was in pain and frankly pissed off. Headwinds, now this... what next?

Ahh yes, the climb. Like many things you fear, it wasn't as bad as I had been imagining, especially after Rimutaka hill. I climbed slow and steady, happy for the brief respite from the headwind. I stopped for a breather to find myself, shamefully, overtaken by another touring kitchen sink type cyclist. Fully loaded he passed me then stopped. He was from Australia and muttered something about the headwinds, then said 'the rain is coming, I need to get to St Arnaud,' and off he went. His legs going round with singular effective monotony. I didn't want a repeat of the Bo cycle hopping incident, so stood there and stuffed down a breakfast bar and let him get far enough ahead then recommenced my climb, it took a while but I eventually topped out and as if by magic the rain started falling. Drizzly, not downpour variety, it didn't last too long and the mainly down hill to St Arnaud was accomplished by 15:00 despite the resumption of the headwind.

It was decision time and I went into the cafe with a lodge opposite and sat pondering my options. It was late, the headwind could worsen, I had already used up reserves of energy I didn't think I had and to make it worse, torrential rain was pouring down. As I sat there a group of germans sat at the same table, two of whom lived here, the others visiting. We got chatting and I asked about the road to Murchison. Hilly but nothing major, nothing like what you've gone over so far. The rain stopped and suddenly I saw my phoenix take off... Fuck it, Im going to do it!

I set off at 15:40 and soon was on the road by myself again. It had opened up into a beautiful valley, mountains at the end, the sun shining down on the glistening road ahead, gently sloping downhill. Suddenly I was overcome with the beauty of it all, and thoughts of all my friends suffering with quiet courage in their battle with Cancer... Mike, Dave, Eira, Sara. Before I knew it tears were pouring down my cheeks even as I was practically shouting 'Fuck it' above the slightly gentler headwind. My legs went round faster as the childlike idea took hold that if I could get to Murchison, complete

100 miles on this day, then all my friends would be ok and Cancer would not win... if only I could get to Murchison. Tears are falling down my cheeks as I write this because I know that such thoughts are not part of the reality of cancer, but in those moments I believed. Fuck it juice coursed through my veins and gave me strength to keep turning the pedals, faster and faster, essentially running on empty, but finding the strength from the example of my friends.

The road ran round the hills following the course of the river, dipping and climbing with the shadow of the phoenix above me .., my fuck it juice lasted well into 15 miles and then started running out. The gorge and the road were something else, running through dark green covered hills with the river thundering down the valley, at times far below, at times right next to me. I crossed the river several times on narrow bridges and the road kept running along the side of the hills. With 20 miles to go, the rain came, drizzly at first, then bucketing it down. Someone might have well thrown several bucket challenge worth over me. It would have had the same effect. Still climbing then descending, fuck it juice ran out and then it was a battle to the death.. or at least total exhaustion. I could barely see out of my glasses, but didn't want to remove them as rain in the eyes at speed is far worse. Fortunately there were few cars and even fewer lorries. Eventually the road turned and headed towards Murchison, the final 6 miles.

Those six miles lasted forever. The road had flattened out and I thought I was going a decent pace but it took forever. Past the Murchison motor lodge (no cabins) and eventually the town sign appeared. I had promised myself I'd stop at the first sight of accommodation and begged the cycling gods to let there be a vacancy. There was... bloody hell, I'm here!

Shower and heater on full blast to begin the drying out process. A phone call from Lorraine (thankyou) to check I hadn't drowned, then a nice meal of nachos loaded with beef mince, cheese, sour cream, washed down with ginger beer.

It has been an epic day. The wind has blown away all my words except for these. I have given everything I am and have to the road today.... if you appreciate my efforts and feel you can sponsor me, please go to www.justgiving.com/GoWithTheCrazy. (*For anyone reading this now the journey has finished - a donation can be made to Love Hope Strength via Just giving at:* https://www.justgiving.com/lhsf)

LHS X

Of all my musings... it seems Fuck it juice inspired more than others... one person suggested I bottle it and sell it... if only!

I was trying to explain the feeling that coursed through my veins - one of complete abandon - like throwing dice and blindly accepting the outcome. In this case it was tied to a feeling I described as childlike - mainly because of the innocence it suggested. Of course it wouldn't make any difference to the battles my friends were fighting - again if only ... Is all I am doing is turning the pedals... the Road doesn't care... Cancer doesn't care - but it was nice to believe it - even if only for that small piece of time. After all I wear Hope on my wrist permanently...

Headwind - the bane of all cyclists. It is written in the cycling laws by those fickle cycling gods...
If there is a flat road... there must be wind...and if there is a cyclist on that road... it is set in stone that it must be a headwind. There is nothing so demoralising as putting all energy and effort into turning round the pedals only to watch your speedometer resolutely stick to single digits. The advantage of a headwind is that it makes you look forward to 'uphill' because there, the wind makes little or no difference.. oh the irony.

Day 18
Hardland ripped and torn apart

The rain was coming down in torrents, no deluge... no ... in biblical proportions... and I'm not exaggerating much. All night it had hammered down as as I peered out my window into the early morning gloom.. yup you've guessed it.... still raining.

My plan then was too set out a little later.. see if the rain would abate somewhat as it had yesterday. I had the 'luxury' of only 54 odd miles today on what should be an easy run (curse that thought... the cycling gods are listening) and therefore felt I could afford a bit of time.

I was extremely tired, worn out after the exertions of yesterday. Everything hurt. I had a lump on my spine from where my rucksack has been bashing... mildly sunburnt legs... knees that felt like those of an 80 year old.... sore arse... and generally totally body tired. The thought of heading out to do battle in that rain was not an appealing one... yet I hauled myself up and packed up, the routine so practised that I was still done and out the door by 07:30 despite my avowed intent to procrastinate.

Once again.. I had ensured everything was carefully waterproofed and today decided to add my leg warmers to my cycle apparel. I was wearing basel layer, cycle shorts and jersey, shorts, leg warmers, rain jacket, windproof gillet and my buff. In short, pretty much all the cycling clothing I was carrying.

The short hop across the road to the cafe was enough to get me damp and somewhat cold.

I ordered pancakes with berries and bananas and my now customary chai latte and sat watching the rain hit the ground hard. Once breakfast was finished.. I sat undercover outside with my bike watching the rain, every now and again becoming convinced it was lightening up, only for the rain to increase in intensity. The fact that I was sitting next to my bike contemplating going out drew many comments from passers by. One lady said if her car wasn't full, she'd offer me a lift. We got talking and I asked her about the road to Reefton. No real climbs, winds its way through the gorge and then flat down SH69 came the reply.

By 08:30 the rain still hadn't slowed so I decided to just go for it... otherwise I could be waiting all day! Deep breath and out I went.. immediately wet. Yet it wasn't so bad... once wet you cant get any wetter and the roads were pretty much deserted. A short climb out of the town and then I was back into the gorge... the road snaking around the foot of the hills high above the river. Flat would not be a word to describe it... but the rises and falls of the road were all pleasantly manageable. And it was stunning scenery. I was surrounded by green... ferns, palm trees.. it had a jungle like feel. And far below the river carved its way with tremendous force... swollen with the recent heavy rainfall. At the side of the road were waterfalls crashing down the hillside, following channels under the road before falling down to add to the river. I was enjoying myself.

The first 20 miles were like this ... only the ups became steeper. Not of epic proportions by any means but to my legs every rise in the road suddenly became a mountain pass and my legs were spinning round but not generating any power at all. Empty... totally fried... bonking big style. I kept stopping to shove sweets and breakfast bars in my mouth... to no avail. And what had seemed an easy run... suddenly became an absolute grind. The scenery distracted a little for the most part but it didn't help that every time I stopped I was swarmed by horrible biting flies. An introduction to the sand fly perhaps.? This ensured that my stops were brief and pushed me onwards.

At one point on a climb up... my legs just gave out. I walked my bike to the top of a climb and found a 'scenic lookout point' complete with bench. It was time for a roll and brie, slightly more substantial than wine gums. As I stood there preparing brunch, in the rain of course, several cars stopped and disgorged their occupants, briefly it turned out, because no sooner had they looked at the view then they decided it was too wet, hopped back in their cars, and drove off. They missed the rainbow... arching over the river... only barely discernible ... but quite an uplifting sight. Food eaten.. back on the road to continue to grind out the miles. My first aim for the day was a little place at the junction of SH6 and SH69 where I would turn towards Reefton for the last 20 miles. Although it seemed an age in coming... I reached it before 12:00 and my dreams of the past 30 miles came true. A cafe... open... serving hot food and drink!! I had thought it possible but had hardly dared to hope and had set myself up for disappointment. I stashed my faithful bike under the overhanging roof and went in... ordered chips and battered sausage and sank gratefully into a chair.

Still raining of course... once lunch was finished I set out again... knowing that the road was deemed to be flat from here too Reefton... and for once... it was true... which is just as well. The gorge had given way to deserted fields in another River valley. I said goodby to the Buller River that had been my not so silent companion for the past two days and followed another river as it wound its way, somewhat more calmly that the Buller River, down the valley. I was crawling along.. every mild rise in the road causing me to crash down into granny gears. I knew I would make my destination, that wasn't a concern, but reaching it as quick as possible was, to allow my legs a bit more recovery time ready for tomorrows longer stage.

It was no use... no matter how much I implored my legs... they weren't listening. They turned the pedals, indifferent to my minds urging. I even had a light tailwind... yes TAILWIND... which again is just as well. If I had been hit with a headwind at this point... I probably would have got out my bivvy bag and curled up by the side of the road.

By 1400 I had ten miles to go. The school bus sign had appeared and signs of civilisation appearing. Adding to my woes... my headphones had died... leaving me with no music to soothe my troubles... leaving me to hear the sound of my chain squeaking(need more oil) and the sound of my wheels on the treacle tarmac. 6 miles to go... still no sight of the town... 4 miles to go... am I ever going to bloody get there... 2 miles... WHERE is the bloody place... 1 mile... Town sign in the distance. Woohooo! Reefton.. The town of light. Apparently because it was the first place in the southern hemisphere to generate its own electricity for public use in 1888, including street lighting.

At that point I really didn't care about bloody street lighting... I needed a place to stay... food and go shopping for provisions and way more importantly for headphones and mosquito spray.

I was going to aim for the Old Nurses home accommodation but to be honest... cool as that would have been... I swung into the first motel I saw. Asked about a vacancy... then cheekily a discount. Yes to both and was shown to 'the cottage' ... a sweet... somewhat old fashioned 2 bedroomed place.. with living room, kitchen and even a washing machine!

I spread my stuff out to dry... changed and went to explore. 4 square supermarket and stocked up including the all important bug spray... but no headphones... agggghhhhh! Directed to an electrical shop and panic over.
Seriously would have been in a bad mood without music!

Then pub... food... and then back to the cottage. The electric fire on (I was bloody cold after todays continuous soaking) and then I crashed out... for hours!!

Leaving me writing this blog at midnight lol.

Have been unable to load photos for the day so will try again tomorrow... something to do with the network connection... which is impossibly slow around here... even with my own personal hotspot.

So here is hoping for a better leg day tomorrow. Day 18 done... the dream is still alive!

From the title of the blog - it would seem like I had a tough day. I guess this is where having a hugely bad memory can be a good thing, as I remember none of the pain. Instead I remember the river crashing through the gorge with so much power, I remember the greenery on either side of me, and the fresh smell emanating from it. (I do also remember the bloody biting insects that made rest impossible!) I remember the relief and the simple joy of having a hot shower and food and the unbridles joy when I found a pair of headphones. All very simple things but imbued with one important lesson for life. Pain is temporary.....as much pain and suffering as I endured in the day, that memory is the quickest to fade and the joy of the simple things in life is held in memory for longer. It is also a truism of life that you can only appreciate the little things when you have faced pain and suffering and that there is always something to be grateful for.

I also loved the way towns in New Zealand had little ways to identify themselves out of the other towns... in this case 'the town of light'. It seemed to be a big thing here and great care goes into choosing the description... I took joy in reading them along the way and there were some good ones... some that made me chuckle, some that made me want to know more about the history of the place. Top prize however goes to Dunedin - for its honesty.... 'It's all right here' which sounds like 'it's ok, I suppose'...

Day 19
It's alright...It's ok

I've been waiting a looonng time to use this as my blog title.. some of which will be explained later in the blog.

Last night I crashed out really early having had difficulties uploading photos to fb. I then awoke at around 23:30 with a blog still to do. By the time I'd finished it was 0100 hours and meant I only got 4 and a bit hours kip overnight. To say I had difficulty waking up this morning was an understatement. By the time I'd hauled my sore arse out of my nice warm bed.. I had very little time to pack up. I initially didn't want to look out of the window and see what the weather was doing but as the time came to make a choice about cycle clothing, I pulled back the curtains to find a grey day with the cloud hanging round the hills.... but no rain!!!

I packed up pretty quickly after that.. dispensed with the leg warmers but kept the gillet. And set off in search of breakfast, literally 2 secs down the road to the pub id eaten the night before. They did a good breakfast but I couldn't drink the coffee which was far too strong for me. I was on the road shortly before 0800.

I had been told that there was a a short climb out of Reefton but then it was pretty flat until Hoikitiki. Just 10 miles from my destination of Ross. Lets go then! So happy not to be drenched the moment I set foot outside.. I joined SH7 for the climb out of Reefton.. and it was fine. My legs were working ok! Ok so the sun wasn't shining but there was no wind and as I crested the hill all I could see was a long straight road, flat by anyone's standards.

The clouds were just hanging in the sky above the hills and it was not cold.
It was around this time my long awaited Its alright .. Its ok plan came into action. Back in January when I was staying with Nicola

and David Johnston I had seen a video they had done during their eight peaks in eight day challenge for LHS. I implored them to put it onto fb, but was met with good natured but absolute refusal! So I did a deal... if I posted a video of me singing Its alright.. its ok on the road in NZ they would post theirs... we even shook on it. Since being on the road all my attempts have been thwarted.... you couldn't hear anything on my action cam above the noise of the road...then it ran out of battery and now it won't switch on. I have tried three times to make a bad video and this was my avowed aim for the day. With my action cam out of action, I decided to instead use my mobile with one hand whilst steering with the other. It required a quiet flattish road, and look what I had in front of me!!!

It was hard to sing and cycle and video all at once, but I was bloody well going to do it this time! And the result is up on my page, never one to mind making a fool of myself - this was for a greater cause...so Nic and David... I expect a video in reply!

Once on the flat SH7, even possibly with a tailwind, I was motoring along, past rivers, and streams, creeks and culverts.. each with their own name.. Deadman creek, flowery river, little grey river and the weirdly named Hou Hou and little Hou Hou rivers. It kept me entertained anyway. With no rain, a favourable wind and speeds of almost 20mph, I was ecstatic. So much so, the singing continued. I was in my element and the legs felt bloody good.

Not totally in the middle of nowhere, with a few farms dotted about, the road was practically my own and I found myself in reverie.. thinking about what might be. I allowed myself to begin dreaming of actually getting to Bluff and how that might feel, then stopped myself as its still a ways off. I turned my thoughts to my day off at the Franz Joseph glacier and my helihike, now within touching distance.. and my tree hut luxury for 2 nights! First though I had 88 miles to cover today, followed by a mere 68 tomorrow.

I also bumped into Jacob, another cyclist, who had crossed the Haast pass in the deluge of the other day. Chapeau!! He was from Poland and doing a Christchurch to Christchurch route around the South Island. We swapped road stories for a good 15 minutes, and it was another encounter that added to what was turning out to be a wonderful day!

My first target today was Greymouth, a town at the joining of SH7 and SH6. Despite going well, the miles started to drag a little. A few hills popped up, nothing my legs couldn't handle but made harder by slipping gears, a pain when you are trying to set a rhythm upwards. Fortunately it was a small annoyance. Then the drizzle started and I settled myself in for a wet ride, but it was not to be.. as the rain cleared again and the skies became less grey. I stopped 2 hours into the ride, treated myself to an ice cream and a blueberry muffin, feeling happy with the ride so far.

It was a good few miles to Greymouth and it took a while to get there. I was aiming for 12:00 but due mainly to photo stops, it was going to be a little slower than that. The mountains started appearing in the distance and they were calling to me, challenging me to go and do battle. I could hear it in my soul.
But that was for another day.

The last 5 miles into Greymouth were upwards round the hills, not bad but I could feel myself starting to tire. A slight headwind had also kicked up, making it harder work than before and reducing my speed to 12-14mph. Eventually the school bus sign appeared, followed by the speed reduction signs and then finally the town sign. It was 12:30! Time for lunch. I found a nice little cafe and to my delight, they served pasta, chicken and spinach variety.. perfect and put the grin back on my face. Lunch done and a few photos, my next aim was Hoikitiki.. it dawned on me what a long day it was as I'd already done around 40 miles and still had the same amount to go, if not slightly more. And whilst on the subject of mileage, yesterday I passed the 1000 mile mark!!!

The headwind kicked up, but as a bonus, the sun was out, not too hot, but so nice. The sea was to my right, waves crashing against the shore, the sky was blue, the mountains in the distance to my left... it was very serene. One bridge I crossed over had a bike path which enabled me to stop and take pictures of the stunning inlet. Difficult to describe, it once again put a huge smile on my face and as I stood there and breathed the air, I felt at total peace with the world. It was that calm!

The road stuck close to the coast, providing a side headwind for me to push against, fortunately it was only a mild one. On this stretch I also saw two cyclists with backpacks and mountain bikes following the cycleway but more of them later! Hoikitiki eventually came into view and I stopped to stock up on calories and I found Hershey's cookies and cream. My staple treat on Route 66, it made my day to sit outside the garage and devour a whole bar on the spot!!

On the road again and I was expecting a climb up to a plateau before descending into my final destination of Ross, but in reality it was an almost imperceptible drag up and accomplished with ease. Then it was put the metal to the pedal time to complete the last 15 miles in good time. When I reached Ross, the gold town, there didn't appear to be much here. Motel, a pub and a few shops. I went to the motel to enquire... just a double left.. discount? Why yes of course, so massive thanks to Kay at Ross motels for her generosity. As we went back to the office the two cyclists I'd seen earlier pulled up, fortunately with a reservation as I'd just taken the last room. And it was a very nice room, meant for at least 2 people but could comfortably hold 3-4 with a large living area and leather sofas... luxury indeed!

The two cyclists, Wiebke and Nigel, live in somerset and are keen bike racers. They were out here mountain biking some tracks for three weeks and driving in between. Coincidently they'd been on the same ferry as me though in a car, which is why I hadn't clocked them. Once showered and changed I set off to the pub for food and they came and joined me. It was lovely to have company, especially people that could talk bikes till the cows came home and we swooped stories, and they gave me some ideas for future explorations... we discussed mountain bikes (Tour Divide in mind) and the inevitable chammy cream conversation. All the while tucking into a well done steak with chips and salad. Nearly 2 hours passed and I had a lovely evening, so thank you to you both and I will be keeping an eye out for the Swedish lake race!!

And so .. its been alright,... its been ok.. in fact its been a downright marvellous day with perfect cycling conditions and having

144

met some wonderful people... and now I have the joy of watching Dave and Nic's video!!

But there are still hard days to come and the mountains laid down the gauntlet to my soul, calling me to go and play...

Thank you to everyone for the support! It keeps my legs turning the pedals for sure. Not wanting to sound like a broken record but at the end of the day this is what it is all about...

If you are enjoying the blogs and feel you are able to sponsor me.. please go to www.justgiving.com/GoWithTheCrazy (*For anyone reading this now the journey has finished - a donation can be made to Love Hope Strength via Justgiving at:* https://www.justgiving.com/lhsf)

Thank you to everyone who has done so already.. we are fighting back together!

It's alright ..It's ok had passed into legend for me Nicola and David... they did indeed post their version up as a reply and I remember laughing out loud.. it completed the day for me so thank you to them both for being such good sports. For those of you that told me not to give up my day job after hearing my version... don't worry it's not going to happen.
The song goes like this - for those of you who don't know it... or those who couldn't hear the words as I belted them out whilst wobbling along...

In the end it's you and me and no one else
This is the way of life
It's alright, it's O.K.
We can make it through tomorrow
It's alright, it's O.K.
There is no one left to follow
In the end for you and me it's now or never
This is the way of time
It's alright, it's O.K.
We can make it through tomorrow
It's alright, it's O.K.

In the above lyrics - beyond the laughter created by me Nicola and David being silly - is a greater meaning.. at least this is how I read it.. other's may interpret it differently... such is the beauty of music and lyrics...

At some point in your life you may be required to fend for yourself.. there will be no one else you can turn to (no one left to follow) and you will have to forge your own path but it will be alright and you will survive through whatever tomorrow throws at you...

At the time of the video production however, I confess, there was no higher purpose or meaning, I just wanted to see if David and Nicola would stick to their bargain and hoped that I could make a few people giggle at my antics!

Day 20
Trying to get to the end of the world….

....Trying to reach the final third
Whenever I fall down you pick me up
Whenever I fall to pieces
You put me back together

So so very tired... last night I had the spins from sheer exhaustion... never a good thing... not a drop of alcohol in sight. Therefore this morning I was somewhat slow to jump out of bed again. Nonetheless... with my now highly honed packing routine I was still out the door by half seven and round the corner hoping... but expecting disappointment as it was Sunday... that it would be open this early. Luck was on my side and breakfast of pancakes on the cards.

The weather... dry... although had rained overnight... still cloudy and a bit chilly. But no rain.. 2 days on the trot... what did I do to deserve that!

The gillet went on but in anticipation... so did the suncream and a herbal fly repellant that may or may not work. What with those... deep heat ... chammy cream and Bepanthen... my life is full of lotions and potions... just gotta be careful and not put deep heat where chammy cream goes! And as for order... do I put on suncream then insect repellant or vice versa?? Answers on a postcard!

Apparently the road ahead (which is forever calling) has a few lumps and bumps in it and one climb of note and then flat to Franz Joseph... my destination and home for my rest day tomorrow. So I set off and braced myself for 67 miles in the saddle. The first 5 miles was relatively flat with not a breath of wind... the roads were extraordinarily quiet and it was looking to be a good day. Then the lumps and bumps appeared. 20 miles of up... down... up ... down... hopping from one scenic reserve to another through the greenest verges of bush I have ever experienced. The crickets were out in force and the birds joined in. I amused myself (it doesn't take much after all these days on the road) by whistling back at them... only to get a reply or two... well it amused me!

The constant up and downing was extremely wearing and it shows what a knifedge Im on in terms of my body packing up. It didn't take long at all (despite the calories I have been shoving in) for the legs to start to blow up on the climbs... the downs not being enough recovery. Grinding out the miles and giving myself a pep talk. Its only 67 miles... 20 done by 10:00... 40 by 12:30 (half hour for lunch) and 67 done by 15:30! Ambitious yes and not allowing any time for photo and snack stops. It was never going to be correct so add on an hour and should be done by 16:30 ... more realistic for sure. These calculations are an ongoing dialogue in my head as I go along... every time I stop.. I recalculate. This takes up a huge amount of thinking time.

I hardly saw a soul on this stretch of road.. I was alone and despite the bad legs was greatly appreciating the solitude... just me and the road. And what a road... winding round and up and down the base of the foothills it was beautiful in its apparent remoteness. The view across the valley was good.

Then came Mount Hercules!!

The climb of the day... I hadn't been particularly dreading it... my new mantra being 'it cant be as bad as The Rimutaka Hill'! The first part was pretty steep but then the gradient eased off and I tapped my way up.. not quite in the lowest granny gear. It was a test but not an insurmountable one.. or even close and it felt good to get to the top. I did think it ironic that this was 'Mount' and Rimutaka was 'hill'... possibly the kiwi sense of humour coming into play. The downhill was fast and flowing and beautiful. I did stop once to let a tour bus through but it was a very pleasant 10 minutes of descending.

As I emerged from those hills I stopped for more calories and found a perfect spot. The valley stretched out with the river at its heart... To my left and in front of me... the hills were getting more mountainous and stretched out of the ground.. reaching for the blue sky. The clouds had cleared except for those shrouding the hills and the sun was trying to break through. Down in the valley... the cows grazed peacefully. It was pretty perfect.

Couldn't last forever though... I could stand around all day but that wouldn't get me to where I wanted to go. So I continued round. Somewhat annoyingly the road twisted round the valley... i kept thinking how much easier it would have been to cut straight across. The wind had also picked up slightly and as the road meandered round... it was a sidewind then headwind then sidewind... (course not a tailwind ... that would be too nice)

I reached a layby where several cars were stopped. The high peaks of the alps were just visible above the thin white cloud. At last... the mountains reveal themselves. I was chatting to one guy who worked for a helicopter company and as we were talking .. one took off and lazily spun round and headed for the peaks... graceful in its manoeuvrability .. the sound of the rotors deadened by space and distance. I spent 5 minutes staring at the peaks and felt like New Zealand was gradually revealing itself to me... as a reward for how hard I'd worked to get here.

At one point I crossed the Kakapotahi River.. narrow bridge but no traffic so for once I allowed myself a bridge stop. The water was grey blue in colour and stretched up to the foothills cutting a gash in the hillside. I resisted the urge to just go and sit on the riverbank forevermore but it mesmerised me and once again I found myself fighting back tears... not usually quite so emotional... it had been a hard road to get here... and this little moment ... in this place... had tipped me over the edge (another knifedge). Weariness may have had something to do with it... but also disbelief that I was standing here... having been convinced many times that I wouldn't get past Auckland.

I breathed the air and absorbed the sounds and smells... trying to draw strength from the natural world around me. Letting it soak into my soul.

As I continued on... the headwind became fiercer... making me fight for every inch of ground gained. Another 5 miles or so and Lake Lanthe came into view. A glorious blue and another oasis of calm until I passed the recreation area with !people!. I continued on.. unwilling to spoil the solitude. Headwind ... sidewind... headwind!! The legs were giving out. The road was relatively flat now with the odd rise but still going slowly ... Fortunately reasonably soon I came across the town of Whataroa and found a cafe... lunch!

I ordered a cheeseburger... devoured it in seconds and then immediately ordered another one!! As I was about to leave a couple of kitchen sink tourers pitched up but unusually for once.. I didn't feel like swapping road stories. I was having a me and the road day and continued on... eager to get to Franz Joseph.

The headwind had worsened... of course... no easy miles allowed. The cycling gods were making me work hard to get to my rest day but I reasoned that nothing worth having is easily won and the pedals kept turning... just! The last ten miles continued in that fashion. Passing two Lakes... both deep blue and calm... more soul fortification. Then buildings started coming into view... Franz Joseph machinery... Franz Joseph holiday park... and then!!! The town sign. I leaned my bike against it and took my photos. Somewhat in shock! I had made it here. The ride is one thing... my rest day here with helihike was the one thing I had on my 'must do' list. I almost had that pinch yourself feeling! These dreams are coming true...

Sauntering towards the town I had a quick mosey before heading to my two nights of luxury accommodation... The Rainforest Retreat and my tree hut. The girl checking me in was from Tilehurst in Reading which really made me laugh and they had kindly given me a 50% discount. I was shown to my tree hut... huuugggee bed... kitchen... nice shower and a balcony!! Perfect... although to be honest... long as it has a bed and electrical sockets it doesn't actually make much difference.

Then I had a treat in store. Some relatives of a friend of my mum (Thanks Rosie for putting me in touch with them... and you must must come here... it's an unbelievable place!!!) were driving over from near Christchurch... just to visit me. Chuffed to pieces... I went to meet them in reception where we relocated to the bar to get a drink before dinner. Mary and Alec were from the UK but now live here near their grandchildren. And it was wonderful to meet them! Mary presented me with two presents... a bag of sweets... and some chafing cream!!! Wooohoooo. Yup I was ecstatic... starting to run out of supplies of 'Udderly smooth' .. it was perfect... as I couldn't see where I was going to find some more. Chammy cream sorted. The conversation flowed... Mary had been a nurse and worked in Reading and Oxford so we swopped stories.. hers of Battle Hospital and the adult wards... turns out she knew some people that one of my work mothers remembered... small world! Did I say how lovely it was!! We then went to eat... and I found Pasta!!!!! The day had a perfect ending... fantastic company and good food... what more could a weary cyclist want. Many hours passed and it was soon time to part company. Despite feeling exhausted I was reluctant to say goodbye to Mary and Alec... a little slice of home...

Thank you so much for coming to meet a strange and slightly crazy cyclist... it was lovely to meet you and you coming all this way to see me is greatly appreciated.

The internet connection wasn't great here and found myself frustrated trying to catch up with facebook and blog... nothing except messenger properly working. I was sitting in bed when I felt a shudder.. the building rocked. Was it??? Could it possibly be??? I had missed the mornings 4.4 earthquake when on the road... but now I excitedly messaged Lorraine.... was there just an earthquake?? 3.7 came the reply!! Woohooooooooooo! Stupidly excited (possibly a bit wrong) to have felt my first earthquake... and I mean really stupidly excited... Lorraine informed me that my Kiwi experience was now complete.

Unable to blog etc I finally crashed out... like lightening... with dreams of tomorrows helihike to the forefront!

I made it here!! And like my blog title says... I'm trying to get to the end of the world but have got here because of all my friends and family picking me up and putting me back together. I couldn't have got this far without your support for sure. The mountains still challenge me to do battle in the days to come but today I am at peace in the beauty of my surroundings.

The mountains calling to me may be an interesting concept and one that has to be felt to be appreciated. I am not built to be a conquerer of mountains on a bike. As previously explained I am no Marco Pantani or Nairo Quintana ... and I struggle when the gradient goes up (need more practice I hear you say). But yet the mountains call their challenge to me and I feel excitement at the thought of pitting myself against their uncaring slopes. It's a call that I can still hear now - tempting me towards ever harder challenges, filled with more climbs... why is that. Well for one - as stated above - Nothing worth having is easily won! The struggle makes the reward so much greater. the reward in this instance being stunning views, the beating of the challenge and I guess the feeling that you are physically capable of completing such a task. All that without the adrenaline rush of the downhill. So for all my moaning about 'uphill', it's in the quest for the reward and in my case inevitably in answer to the call of the mountains. And if you listen carefully - you may hear it too! (Ashley and Kristine, the Ben is calling to you!)

Franz Joseph itself was a town I shouldn't have like, but did. It was touristy and tacky in places. Tourist shops and signs advertising all the different activities you could take part in. I hate towns, the more touristy, the worse they generally are. But Franz Joseph felt different. It had a clean vibe, youthful even, where it felt like the possibilities were endless. It had an air of vitality and seemed to shout at you to get going and take advantage of the opportunities that nature held for enjoyment. It's quite possible that I'm overstating it, my view blinded by weariness and joy at reaching this place, that had been a goal and a reward for all the energy I had expended out on the road. Weariness was displaced by rising excitement at what my 'rest day' would hold and what sights I would see.

Some of the people I spoke to the following day who lived and worked in the town told me that Franz Joseph had a hold on them and many others that came here, intending to work for a season or two and were still planning to leave 5 years later. Understandably, the winter season was quiet and dull for many of them, yet they either stayed or came back year on year. the scenery might have had something to do with it... or the freshness of the air... or the aforementioned vibe of the place but having stayed for just 2 nights, I could understand.

Mary and Alec made my arrival all the more sweeter and enjoyable. Strangers to me, but nonetheless from home and it soon felt like we had known each other for a long time. I can't thank them enough for welcoming me into Franz Joseph and their company at various points of my stay there. I'm so glad to have met you and shared a part of my journey with you.

Day 21
I'm made of life

I woke up at 7am after a lie in! It seemed like a silly thing to waste the day sleeping. I did stay in bed and chill for an hour or so before heading into the town to mooch about and find breakfast. I checked out the wildlife place with the intention of seeing a kiwi... $35 for what seemed like a very short experience. I walked out again .. hoping to go back later. I wandered into the souvenir shops... fortunately I am limited in what I can carry which means I'm limited to postcards and fridge magnets and my bank balance isn't under too much threat. Generally here prices were high as it was a 'tourist trap'... but a nice one. Franz Joseph has a nice bustling vibrant vibe to it..perhaps drawing its energy from the mountains behind.

And what a panorama awaited me today. The cloud had cleared... the sun was out .. sparkling off the snow on the peaks of the Southern Alps. For some reason.. cloud I think... I hadn't seen the mountains when I arrived yesterday... but it was like the cycling gods had said.. 'well done for getting here... here is your reward'!

Having done my shopping I decided to go for breakfast and wandered into a cafe with a mountain view... I wanted to soak up as much of the view as possible and imprint this day on my memory. As I was taking a seat I heard my name... turned round... and to my delight ... it was Mary and Alec! Having stayed at Fox Glacier, where there wasn't anything open.. they came here and we just so happened to choose the same place to eat. It was a lovely unexpected surprise for the day and we sat chatting whilst I devoured pancakes... again!

Eventually though it was time to say goodbye again and I waved them off and turned my attention to the day to come. This was the one day I had booked accommodation and had been determined to get to. I moseyed on over to the Glacier guides base. As I did so I passed a kiosk for Lake Kayaking and on a whim.. went in to enquire. As luck would have it... they had one space for an evening

Lake tour and with very little hesitation I booked myself in! You only live once right... rest day be dammed!

Then it was booking in time. A slight mix up meant that my flight time was 15 minutes later than I had thought it would be and it was going to be cutting it close to get back for the kayak... but couldn't be helped and I just kept my fingers crossed for no delays. The group I was with, held some surprises. On the website .. this trek, Ice Explorer, had been advertised as reasonably strenuous with three hours of walking on the glacier... those without a good level of fitness were advised to go for the helihike version.. with less walking around on the ice. As I surveyed the group there were two older people, who looked less than steady on their feet on the flat! Yup guilty of pre judging but I was a little surprised. I had expected the younger people to be on this one. Instead they all seemed to be doing the hike to the glacier!

We suited and booted.. with all kit provided. Just as well because I cant carry boots and walking kit but I didn't like wearing boots that weren't my own... and though they seemed to fit it could cause problems. We were assigned seats in the helicopter having been weighed. I didn't get the front unfortunately but was determined to get a window seat on the way up!

We walked along a jungle path to the helipad and watched as several helicopters landed and flew off with groups like our own. Then it was our turn. Excitement at a screeching level to match the noise of the helicopters rotors we lifted off and turned before climbing up and heading towards the hills. Briefly the thought of the heli crash at Fox glacier went through my mind but was quickly dismissed as the glacier came into view. White ice tumbling towards the valley floor.. flanked by ice that was brown with the debris from the mountainside. As we approached ... the size of the glacier and the ice formations became apparent. The people already on the ice were specks in the vast ice field. The helicopter landed softly on the ice platform and we disembarked... the noise echoing round and the rotor wash doing its best to blow us off our feet. We walked up past other groups with big grins on their faces and our guide Nick got us corralled together to put our crampons on. He introduced us to our other guide Nick (makes that easy) and before long we were all standing in a line ready for going up. We were the first people on the ice for 5 days as the weather had been bad and they explained they may have to do some path and step cutting along the way .. two huge axes having been brought along for the purpose. We set off ... the crampons biting into the ice and providing a secure step.

As we went along.. every now and again.. the axes would be swung and bits of ice sprayed.. as the two Nicks cleared the path and re- formed the steps. It was reasonably easy going. Any steep steps and a rope had been fixed with an ice screw. But the older couple were struggling in parts and did slow the group down a bit. I didn't mind as it enabled me to take lots of photos and part of me also thought fair play for coming out and doing this... i hope I'm still doing things like this when I'm their age! They hailed from Colorado and although the steep steps were a bit of a problem.. they managed it and kept up on the flatter sections.

We were basically going up and down ridges of ice... carved out by the glacier movement and shaped by the wind and rain. Every now and again a look back down the valley showed the ice stretching down under the blue sky and a look up to the higher point of the glacier to the more 'unstable part' showed glistening tower blocks of ice ... seracs... ready to topple at any moment. The icefall was breathtaking in its beauty... the blue of the older ice sparkling through in places.

After a good few ups and downs Nick 2 stopped us and invited anyone who felt tired or finding it hard to stay at this point to be collected. I wondered if that was a hint to the older couple but they were determined to continue.

We kept walking until we reached the highest point we were to go. The icefall part deemed too unstable to go in... we stopped below what they call the hole! Appeared in 2008 this gap in the ice is widening quickly and may cause large sections of the glacier to shear off. Nick also pointed out the level of the glacier just 6 years ago and a line was clearly discernible. It has receded a huge amount in that

157

time and although part of the cycle depending on weather systems.. of growth and recession... the last 6 years was more dramatic than previous.

Eventually it was time to head downwards and a small problem worsened. The boots were rubbing on my left heel quite badly and i could feel a sore area. I just hoped it wouldn't ruin the days to come. All too soon, having squeezed through ice cracks and wandered through more beautiful ice formations, we were back at the helipad... crampons off... and waiting for our ride back down the valley. The clouds had closed in making it a bit chilly and it was good to be back in the chopper heading for the warmer valley floor.

On landing... I had about 45 minutes to find a snack and check in for my kayaking trip!!

Checking in done I sat chatting to a young lady called Cesia... from Mexico. She had worked in a motel in Franz Joseph for over a year but had never gone Kayaking and was about to remedy that. Every winter she goes home expecting not to return but something draws her back here.

We piled in 2 minibuses and set off for Lake Mapourika .. a short drive away. Kitting up in the most fashionable spray skirts and jackets was funny and the sand flies took advantage of us standing still... biting wherever they landed. We were soon sitting in our kayaks... paddles in hand ready for the off. I was in the front and Cesia was in the back with control of the rudder ... so I was quite happy as every following crash into bushes and riverbanks was solely her responsibility!!

We slowly paddled across the lake... the early evening sun poking through the clouds and reflecting off the water... reasonably calm to start with... as we went further out it became slightly choppier but still easy paddling. We were aiming for the kiwi reserve at the far side of the lake and the calm of the lake and the evening seeped into me... taking away all the stress on the body of the preceding days and leaving me feeling relaxed and calm. The sound of the water as we carved through it became a soundtrack to just breathing in and out as we made our way across.

Lake Mapourika had once been part of the glacier and as a huge block of ice had carved off and melted.. it had formed the lake. Pretty deep as glacial formed lakes are... the water was extremely clear and a deep blue.

We reached the kiwi reserve and kayaked down a small channel... often becoming 'one' with the bushes on either bank. The reserve is where they breed the rarest kind of kiwi. The young are then flown to an island in the Marlborough sounds where they are safe from predators and then flown back here. They now number above 500. A fantastic programme which I have now contributed to as the kayak company pays the Department of Conservation per kayaker to go there.

The inlet was calm and peaceful and the sounds of the birds calling and the crickets was all encompassing.

Too soon it was time to turn round and go back and we lazily paddled across the lake again in the early evening light. I got talking to one of the guides about the ride. He had heard of the Eastern who are playing at the gig at the end of the ride and was a big fan of them. A climber initially from the UK he had arrived here almost by accident... kept intending to leave but had ended up staying. Though he was 'definitely' going back to the UK in a few weeks.

Soon we washed up ashore... climbed out of the kayaks and found ourselves pretty wet. Transfer back and then race on to get food and start drying out clothes to pack up tomorrow....

Having half forgotten about my bike (sorry bike) the next few days started playing on my mind as I was eating. Only 5 days left but all exceedingly tough ones... I had left the best for last! With the Haast Pass to face and several 80+ mile days... my road to Bluff will not be an easy one!

Please help me keep the pedals turning by sponsoring me if you can .. www.justgiving.com/GoWithTheCrazy. *(For anyone reading this now the journey has finished - a donation can be made to Love Hope Strength via Justgiving at* https://www.justgiving.com/lhsf *)*

Thank you for all your support so far... it keeps the pedals going round.

Despite all the activity today... I feel energised. I'm made of life!

Day 22
Only the Phoenix knows

A bit about this phoenix I keep mentioning...
A mythical creature that rises from ashes...

To me it is my symbol for that which gives me inspiration... hope and strength. It stands for courage to face whatever is ahead. My phoenix flies above me to be summoned when needed. He watches over me.

Sad news from home...

It was a grey morning for many reasons... the cloud hanging over the mountains reflected how I was feeling. Gone were the white peaks of yesterday... hiding in the dense cloud... perhaps knowing that I would not appreciate their beauty today. It was even cold. The rain had held off... perhaps out of respect for the struggle I had inside. I wanted to be at home.

But would it change anything... no!
Some things are not within our control... like headwinds... you just have to accept.... shout and yell and curse all you want... but the wind doesn't care.

And I had a ride to finish...

I set off... rolling up the road and found breakfast. Oh the comfort of routine... packing up... looking at the day ahead... working out how long it would take me... all part of my ritual... distraction from the urge to run away.

Once breakfast was done... eggs and bacon if you must know... I turned my music up loud and began the climb out of Franz Joseph. A gentleman a couple of days ago told me that the three climbs on this day were more to worry about than the Haast pass (tomorrows little jaunt!) so I was wary of how I would go up this first climb...

wondering if my legs would function after my not very restful rest day.

The words of Mike Peters filled my heart and soul as I climbed steadily upwards... taking strength from the lyrics of every song... There are no frontiers... The only limitation is in my mind... only the thunder knows... I breathe the air. I climbed strongly... aware my phoenix was watching me... giving me strength.

The hills.. shrouded in a deep green... surrounded me as I wound around and up. My legs grew stronger as I gained the climbing rhythm (granny gears of course). I was pretty much alone and this stretch of SH6 was bereft of civilisation. Very soon I topped out... hill 1 done and whizzed down the other side in glorious free-fall... sweeping bends... still slightly damp from last nights rain.. taking care not to go in too deep or brake too hard.

This downhill did a bounce and catapulted me up the start of hill 2. An equally tough climb with gradients on the hairpins that would make Alberto Contador wince (slight exaggeration but hey ho) The road absorbed all my concentration .. the next inch of tarmac becoming the most important thing to me... leaving me with no brain power for any other thoughts... legs went round like a metronome set at 45 RPM for the hills. (Thanks for the advice Mike!) At one point I got off and hike a biked round the hairpin... it was just too steep. Then I got back on my bike and began again.

On the way up whilst I was sweating... huffing... groaning and generally looking every inch the crazy fool I am.. I passed two girls walking down the road.. As I passed one of them said... in an American accent... 'You're so badass'. It was the first thing that made me smile all day.

I muttered something like... 'no just stupid' and continued on up.. but a large part of me wanted to go and thank her for making me smile.

Hill number three was easier than hills 1 and 2... though still required a significant amount of effort. All this and I still hadn't reached Fox Glacier yet.. a mere 15 ish miles away.

When I cruised downhill into Fox... I probably should have stopped to replenish water and increase stocks of food. But I hadn't done many miles and time was ticking on... so I whizzed straight through and up the other side.

The whole day to Haast was a total of 87 miles... it was 10:30 and id hardly done any. I hoped the road would get a little easier.

It did flatten out somewhat and as the road was winding around the valley i had descended into... I even occasionally got a tailwind. Id run out of fuck it juice and instead opened the pissed with the world bottle... which gave my legs the strength they needed to really motor... speeds of 17mph were maintained for a short while as all conditions aligned for a brief moment in time and space.

The road after that continued to dip up and down with jungle on either side. Cool streams ran beside the road but I was hesitant to drink the clear running water because I'd seen signs that stated the land had been poisoned to try and kill the possums. Somewhat a controversial subject... some farmers were using a poison called 1080.. whilst others displayed signs saying No to 1080. All very well but I wasn't confident the water was safe to drink. The sun was out in fits and starts though.. and given that I didn't think I'd get a refill until Haast.. my end destination.. I split my options and filled a bottle from the stream .. for emergency use only. Incredibly clear.. with no debris.. it would have otherwise been perfect!

I passed places with names but no services... the nicest being a bay with a beautiful beach.. stopped to take a photo and my legs became black with the swarm of sandflies!! I left pretty quickly!!!

Unbelievably a few miles down the road... I saw a sign for a cafe... at a salmon farm. Like an oasis ... it was a good thing cos I was running out of food and energy and there was still 40 miles to go. There were a few coaches of tourists who stared at me when I parked up my bike and two or three other bikes of the kitchen sink variety parked up. I ordered eggs on toast... my daily cup of chai latte and sat ... swatting off sandflies contemplating the miles to come. I didn't take long and was soon suiting up again. I got chatting with a kitchen sink cyclist ... he had come from Fox and as I was telling him about our ride another guy joined in the conversation. I asked him where he had cycled from and he said he wasn't on a bike... he just liked that particular cycling jersey!

His name was Max and he was from the Netherlands... a photographer of mountains.. he is off to Patagonia next... really quite jealous. Lovely to meet you Max... I look forward to seeing those photos!!

Then back on the road... ahead of the kitchen sink cyclist... determined to stay there but given the state of my legs wasn't sure I could manage it. Then it started to rain!! Fairly heavy but I decided not to put on my rain jacket as 'if you don't like the weather in New Zealand..wait 5 minutes'. Sure enough the rain soon stopped leaving me to contemplate another very hilly stretch. Another 4 longish hills but with a reasonable gradient and a bit of flat in between. The first was ok and I just tapped up it. Coming down I went through a swarm of bees!! Keeping my mouth firmly shut I passed through without incident other than being hit a few times by wayward fliers. I stopped for more food and as I did so kitchen sink guy caught up with me!! Damn. My bike was lighter but as he pointed out... I had way less gears... making it harder. Swings and roundabouts.

He continued on up and I caught him on climb number 2. Going past once again I struggled up this one ... my legs going round a bit faster so as not to get caught again (damn competitive streak) On the third hill.. there was a lookout point halfway up... beautiful vista of the ocean. Stood there and took photos for ten minutes surrounded by coaches of tourists. They all swarmed out of their coaches... took photos and hopped back on the bus. Weird way to see a country in my opinion!

Of course had been caught and passed by kitchen sink... so once again set off after him. Once passed... another bee swarm in the downhill... I bumped into another tourer. He needed some oil for his chain so I dutifully provided some. He had cycled from Slovenia to Singapore and then just kept on going. Admiring my light set up... we chatted for a while... kitchen sink passed me... and then time to go. He informed me that it was flat from here but headwinds all the way to Haast!

He was totally correct... the headwind slowed me down somewhat and were a real struggle. But due to my lighter.. more aerodynamic set up I passed kitchen sink for what turned out to be the last time! Running along the coast... the headwinds were the fiercest I encountered yet and slowed me to 6mph. The beach had golden sand and the sea and sky were bright blue. It was lovely. The sun was out and if it wasn't for the headwind this would have been one of the nicest stretches I've done.

I fought for an hour before finally coming to the Welcome to Haast sign.. and whooopped with delight. Somewhat prematurely it turned out as there was at least another 5 miles to go. Fortunately the road turned inland a little and speed picked up a bit. There was a long bridge over the Haast river with two passing places... which meant I could get a photo. The mountains were once again making their presence felt... reminding me of the Queen Stage tomorrow. I battled once again against the headwind over the bridge... cursing all the way until finally in the town. 87 miles done on a very hilly day. Not bad at all.

Motel wise.. the first one I went into was full so tried the backpackers next door... yup had a room and showed me round... then you can bring your bike in... unload your stuff... and put the bike round the back.....

Eerrrrr ... no. He was adamant about the bike... comparing it to a car and pets!!!!!!

So I took myself... and my bike down the road where another motel was. Vacancy ... woohoo. And bike could be 'snuck' in the room. All good then. Dinner of burger and chips and all good except for the wifi. My TEP cant connect as no phone signal so had to pay for very bad wifi... hence no blog till this morning.

As for me.. how do I feel today? Only the phoenix knows...

Day 23
There are no frontiers

This was the big one... the day to end all days. If this was a Tour ..
this would be the Queen's stage... the most anticipated... the hardest...
the one that would see some break and others seize the day! Just over
80 miles and 8750ft to climb. .. over 2000ft more than any other day.

I packed up and was out door... to hopefully find an open cafe...
and luck was on my side. It was just as well because it was a good 50
miles before the first cafe... and that was after the Haast Pass through
the mountains... so I needed food and supplies. Both sorted... and the
rain now falling heavily... I put on all waterproof layers (jacket only)
and set off. Damn it was cold. Half tempted to stop and put the leg
warmers on I decided not to because may be glad of them being dry
later so ploughed on regardless.

The rain was hammering down and I was soon very wet... wet
feet... arms... shorts... completely soaked through. The real climbing
wouldn't start for 20 miles but there was no shortage of ups....
winding round the foothills with the river as a guide... often far
below. There were flat sections and fortunately the tailwind on these
short bits meant my legs weren't completely dead just yet. .. in fact
they were completing the climbs pretty well... but I was very aware
that the real climbing had not yet begun.

Mount Aspiring national Park came up next. Unfortunately the cloud and the rain meant there wasn't much to see. Not that I was in an appreciative frame of mind. My feet were now numb with cold... my hands close to the same. Whenever I stopped there was nowhere to shelter so every now and again I stuffed a tracker bar down and a few sweets and a gulp of water... and set off as quickly as possible.

The worst bit being the wet shorts sticking to the legs until I got going again.

I could see how Mount Aspiring would be stunning in nice weather... the river was a glacial blue/grey in the valley below and high rock walls ran next to the road... well above the river at times... All the foothills that I could see were covered in dense green bush.. and mist and rain and cloud so that mostly just an outline was visible.

Battling the rain and the cold meant my reserves... both mentally and physically were close to zero... I had daydreams about thumbing a lift... but didn't stop near any laybys in case I gave in. I was so cold I had some concern about hypothermia... especially as the road started to wind upwards on a more permanent basis instead of the up and down.

I was concerned about time... it was already half ten and the real climbing was just beginning. Flashbacks to the Rimatuka Hill came and went... it cant be that bad ... can it??

The main problem was that I didn't know what I was really facing... it could be another Rimatuka... it could be worse... it could be better... the mind conjured up scenarios of me still climbing the pass at 4 or 5pm... then what?? Being wet and very cold made it clearly worse and then I passed through the Gate of Haast (gate of hell more like) which signified the start of the proper climbing. 15-20% in places I reckon... with an escape hill on the opposite side of the road... (that tells you how bad it was!).. and gears that were slipping drove me to the very edge of breaking point. I was absolutely certain I wasn't going to be able to finish today... ..

You may not believe how close I was to stopping.. or how desperately I wanted to sit down and close my eyes... be warm and dry at home... or how the tears ran down my face in frustration at myself for being weak...

But something kicked in... and I honestly don't know what it was.... it just kept the pedals turning... even as the thoughts of quitting were shouting to me... the pedals kept turning. If I stopped... I started up again...

I kept going up... so slowly as it was still very steep... then downhill... then another steep climb.... and another...

I couldn't see out of my glasses further than the next foot of tarmac... but maybe that helped...

The steep climbs kept coming... with a little downhill in between... which served to freeze me solid... until I saw a sign... Haast pass... 564m. I had bloody done it. Well... got this far anyway. Shivering I stuffed down more fruit bar things and prepared for a very cold descent. My aim... the cafe.. in 20 miles... It was mainly downhill with a bit of flat and the mountains started slowly receding into the background... the rain slowed to a trickle and some warm air found me!

Suddenly anything seemed possible.. There are no frontiers that we can't cross...

The twenty miles to the cafe were pretty pleasant... with the rain going... a tailwind at times and the scenery becoming more visible... the world seemed a better place.

I sped that 20 miles and found myself at the cafe at 13:40. Much better time than I dared to hope or thought realistic... given how I'd felt going up. But I had conquered the Haast pass in pretty awful weather and emerged with a quiet satisfaction that I hadn't given up even though every fibre in my body screamed for me to do so...

After lunch it was a short drop down to Lake Wanaka and the sun was out... I was quickly drying off and removed my rain jacket to allow other layers to wind dry.

Lake Wanaka... a beautiful blue... ringed with mountains (the peaks of the tallest still hidden by cloud... words cannot describe the beauty other than how it penetrated the soul to leave it bewildered.

The road wound round the lake neither rising or falling steeply... leaving me with energy to spare to gaze at it as I wound round it. Then the road started climbing again... i could see it in the distance make a break for the gap in the hills to jump over to Lake Hawea. It was warm now and I had found my climbing legs...

Lake Hawea appeared into view only after I had climbed The Neck... 400 and something feet and it was just as spectacular... only more so ... as it signalled that I would make it tonight. 5 miles to go and they were some of the prettiest... running alongside the Lake in all its glory... Up and down of course... and one absolute bugger of a climb... just to finish me off and twist the knife in a little. To add insult to injury... I was overtaken by a bunch of clowns... !! Literally as the circus was in town and kept passing me on the road!

Drying off as I 'sped along' (everything is relative) I wondered what the car drivers thought as they went from a to b when they saw me. Did they even notice at all??

Soon Hawea.. the town came into view. Never been quite so happy to see a little town.. so I crossed the bridge to the first... and only hotel... fully booked. The kind lady 'phoned a friend' and sent me to see Bev... (It was at this point that I fell asleep whilst blogging last night!)
And I was soon ensconced in a nice room with a hell of a view of the lake... a loo with a view... my cycling clothes in a washing machine and on my way to get dinner at the cafe down the road.

The young lad serving me reminded me of my step son with his inability to finish off a sentence with anything other than 'sweet' and the burger and chips were pretty good but was too tired to finish them.

Back to Bev's and was soon crashed out.. unable to finish this blog I was so tired.

I came close to breaking point yesterday but whatever saw me through meant I am still on schedule and battling to get to the end. I cannot do it without your support.

A massive thank you to everyone who has shared the posts... messaged me and commented on the posts. And an even bigger thank you to everyone who has sponsored me so far... www.justgiving.com/GoWithTheCrazy. (*For anyone reading this now the journey has finished - a donation can be made to Love Hope Strength via Justgiving at* https://www.justgiving.com/lhsf *)*

LHS

The first half of this day was the toughest I had encountered yet. It wasn't so much the climbing but the climbing in combination with the cold and rain made me come to as close to breaking point as I have ever been. But the body and the mind's ability to persevere through huge discomfort and pain and misery is phenomenal and

resides within us all. Pain is only temporary.. as I keep reciting to myself on days such as this... but weakness is permanent. I had been tested by the mountains and beaten them. I had endured. I will face harder tests in my life that require strength of mind and body.. little did I know I would face one when I returned home.. but having faced this test I feel that I have gained more fortitude to help deal with whatever life throws at me. And whatever tests I set myself, whatever challenges I dream up to test my mind and body, others face harder tests in their daily lives and to those people I have nothing but admiration for their courage and strength, which puts mine into proportion.

My one regret is that I didn't get to see Mount Aspiring National Park in all it's glory. Repeatedly described as stunning, I couldn't see it through the buckets of rain lashing down on me and the low cloud which hovered just above my head. However - I was indeed incredibly lucky with the weather on my rest day so on balance I would have chosen that.

Ironically I discovered that a friend of mine, Sue S, was travelling in the opposite direction to me that day - on the same stretch of road. Perhaps fortunately we didn't meet or my resolve may have crumbled with the lift she surely would have offered.

My reward that day was a spectacular view of the two lakes, both literally awe-inspiring in their beauty, especially when compared the murk I had descended out of. Once again, it may have been slightly skewed with my euphoria at making it over the Haast Pass but I have never seen such a beautiful sight.

Day 24
Let it Raindown

I struggled to wake up again this morning... a fact demonstrated by the squeezing onto my toothbrush... of Bepanthen!!!

Fortunately noticing before applying it to my teeth... I cleaned it off and applied toothpaste instead. It didn't have its usual minty taste.

Not a great start... things were looking up with breakfast (thanks Bev) and the news that she had contacted a friend who was a reporter for the Wanaka Times... who wanted to meet me and write an article for the paper. It was arranged for the morning on my way to first Cromwell... then through the gorge to the outskirts of Queenstown. All on SH6... this road that had been with me since Greymouth would carry me all the way to Bluff.

Bev assured me that it was pretty flat from here to Wanaka (definitely the kiwi version of flat Bev!!!!) and the plan was to get there by 08:15.. but on setting off and climbing the hills as they appeared.. my legs weren't in the game this morning and Wanaka town would be a detour too far off route... so I phoned Nicky.. the reporter and she suggested we meet at Puzzletown cafe! A weird place with lopsided buildings and a backwards clock amongst other things. The article will be out after the ride but still hopefully raise awareness...

That done... the road to Cromwell was calling... and what a beautiful road.! Yes some climbs... it is New Zealand... but all manageable... mountains behind and to the sides ... visible across fields burnt golden by the sun.. which was making an appearance every now and again!! I may also have been lucky enough to have a bit of a tailwind at times but was careful not to say it out loud in case the cycling gods realised their grievous error.

There was a lot of thinking done on this stretch... careful not to think too much about arriving in Bluff (stuff can still go wrong) I looked back over the last few weeks which simultaneously have gone by in a flash and also seem like forever ago. In fact .. this morning seems like a long time ago.. never mind the moment when I put my feet in the pedals for the first time here. There are many many highlights ... although it may seem like I moan a lot in my blog... I have already forgotten the pain of the first few days and difficulty breathing and remember instead the lovely sunshine... the rainforest... the golden sandy beaches (still remember the sand flies in Oppononi though) and the people I met along the way... many who left a lasting impression on this journey and some who went above and beyond to keep this cyclists legs turning round!!

Also whilst I remember... have had many enquiries about the state of my hands. Last time after Route 66 .. I couldn't hold a knife and

175

fork... couldn't do up buttons and generally had claws for hands. Im pleased to report that this time hands seem better (the last 2 days notwithstanding). I did get some major hand cramps after kayaking... but they were wet and cold and had been gripping the paddle for a while. The palm of my hand is a bit numb but the fingers seem to be working still. Fingers crossed (pun only half intended) that they continue to be as good!!

So the road to Cromwell went on... I have been told that I have taken the easy way as there was a 'shortcut' from Wanaka to Queenstown but it happens to go over the Crown Range and I for one am incredibly glad I inadvertently chose to go The Long Way Round.

I reached Cromwell in good time ... by 12:00 and found a cafe to shove even more calories down. Just by the cafe... The Large Plastic Fruit!! Had to take a photo to add to my collection of Giant things lol.

The last few miles into Cromwell had been dogged by a bit of a headwind and now as I turned to go through the gorge leading to Queenstown... it became a full throttle headwind... complete with some spots of rain though that held off for a bit. The headwind abated a little allowing me to negotiate the rises and dips of the gorge with little trouble. Nothing major at present I did have the feeling that it was working up to a crescendo...

In the meantime I stared at the turquoise River below as it gouged its way through. This area had had mines in .. as has much of the Otago region...(a fact I learnt from reading a book about cycling the Otago rail trail)... and because I had been forewarned I stared intently at the scarred and broken hillside... and sure enough .. once the eye was in... you could pick out remainders of miners huts dotted about the hillside.

The beautiful blue river was at times calm and tranquil and at other times crashing and fierce but the road continued beside it and above it. Some steeper climbs were starting to test my legs and in particular the one I hoped would be the signal for the road to turn downhill. Granny gears to the fore... I tapped up it and once at the top saw a lady climb away from her camper van and over the barrier...

'Don't Do It!!!'

I did actually shout that... but with a smile on my face and the lady turned round... camera in hand and said 'no thats further up the road' (Turns out it actually was... as the famous bungee jumping bridge is located in this gorge!)

Andrea and Ian were from West Sussex in the Uk and were driving to Cromwell to visit friends on their vineyard. Thank you for giving me a smile and lovely to meet you. I hope you have a safe journey home... who knows we may meet in Chiangi Airport!!!

Then the road started downhill a bit but the headwind had kicked up to vicious proportions and was either straight on or mixed with a sidewind. So bad... I was crawling along on the flat around 4-6mph if not less at times when gusts bought me to a standstill. Downhill bits were becoming dangerous... narrow road and a gusting head/sidewind make for difficult bike handling... then ... yup...

you've guessed it... the Raindown began. Intense enough for me not to wait the usual 5 minutes... I whipped out my rain jacket and prepared to get very wet.

This stretch was about 15-20 miles and should have been done (including climbs and photos in 2 hours max... it took almost double that in the end... such was the strength of the wind.

Soaking wet once again... I struggled onward waiting for the point that the road turned... 7 miles away. Every inch of ground gained was a struggle. I did stop for more calories... sat down by the roadside when three mountainbikers came whooshing past (with a tailwind) on the Queenstown dirt trail that runs next to the road. The third guy... slowed up and asked if I was alright... nice... but it did make me smile... having come over 1400 miles ... is all I was doing was eating... though he would have got a different answer yesterday morning!!

The road turned slightly... after 7-8 very hard fought miles and with the rain still beating down... I picked up a bit of speed... no longer straining to overcome the headwind...

I did shout above the noise of the wind/rain and cars...

Let it Raindown... cos Im nearly fcuking there!!

And boy did that feel good.

Entered Frankton.. on the road skirting Queenstown... past the full motor camp... past the no vacancy b&b and out of Frankton... plan b then. Up a steep hill to Peninsula Road and the Hilton hotel complex... my last avenue before having to cycle another 20 miles.

I rolled up to the grand entrance... literally dripping wet and went in. Only one room left
.. double apartment style $530... hmmmmm Tempting!!

I begged for a discount... explained what I was doing and how far id come... the manager went away to ask his boss and came back with an offer...$279... done deal thank you! So thats how I find myself in the very swish apartment with balcony and resplendent with sofas..

Makes me laugh though cos it makes bugger all difference to me ... long as I have a bed and electrical sockets... I'm good anywhere!

I also managed to Periscope this evening so if you didn't catch it live... it will still be available for a little while at www.periscope.tv/OneChallengeAtATime and you can access by clicking the link above.

I still have 2 days to go... tomorrow to Winton... 96 ish miles... reasonably flat which leaves 40 miles for my last morning to Bluff... where Lorraine will be waiting for the transfer to Dunedin for the gig (massive thanks to Doug and Andy at Auden Guitars!!!).

I'm raising money for Love Hope Strength Foundation and have battered my body and mind into submission in order to be worthy of your sponsorship... if you haven't already and feel that you can... please visit www.justgiving.com/GoWithTheCrazy and help me to the 'End of The World' (*For anyone reading this now the journey has finished - a donation can be made to Love Hope Strength via Just giving at* https://www.justgiving.com/lhsf)

LHS

My hands - vital for my job - it was a source of worry for me. I had done everything I could possibly to mitigate the effects of riding so far for so many days. As mentioned last time I came home with hands resembling a claw... this time, although I had a slight bit of numbness for a few days I could still hold a knife and fork and attach my iPod to my belt. I did suffer from extremely painful hand cramps on my return. My fingers would just straighten and become unmovable, accompanied by a spasm of pain. these too fortunately

179

have generally resided and apart from the odd one, 4 months later no longer trouble me.

So what was different this time... ?

The days were just as long and if anything they were harder with worse cold and rain than in America. I had bar tape on my bars both times and was wearing padded gloves, though this time, if anything, the padding was thinner.

I had added some aero bars onto my bike but because of the terrain (either up or down), there were few opportunities to use them, though maybe the few times I rested on them made all the difference.

An awareness of the need to continuously change my hand position was possibly the difference and I ensured that I changed every 5 minutes or so. I was also conscious if I was holding the bars too tightly and made efforts to loosen my grip, especially when climbing. Every now and again I massaged Deep Heat into my hands which may also have helped though I cannot be sure.

It is an ongoing experiment.. to find a formula that leaves my hands in full working condition or at least hastens the recovery time after rides and I would be very interested in any suggestions that people have. www.facebook.com/OneChallengeAtATime

Day 25
Spiritual Regeneration Every Single Time We Breathe

The second longest day in terms of mileage and coming after 2 long climbing days... this was not an 'easy day'. Im not sure this country has any of those in it. 97 miles but only 2700 ish feet of climbing... this was a wind dependent day... a lot hung on the wind direction and strength.

I admit... I pushed my bike up the hill from the hotel... and if you'd seen it... you would understand why... 20% gradient is a good way to break yourself for the rest if the day... as it was, pushing the bike up that hill hurt!!

I then coasted down and rejoined SH6... having shunned breakfast in the very expensive hotel.. I knew that there was a cafe to be found 25 miles down the road at Kingston... First though I had to go along Lake Wakatipu..
With a bit of road called Devil's Staircase.. this could be bad.

A tailwind pummelled me along to the lake... I hesitated to even think about it... because I knew if it changed... I could be in for a ridiculously hard day. But couldn't complain at the moment... 20mph down a straightish flattish road... with a tailwind for the most part.. perhaps a sidewind at worst.

And then I got to the lake proper and if I have used up all my superlatives previously... please forgive me for repeating myself. The Remarkables mountain range to my left were ... simply... remarkable. The Lake was a beautiful blue.. only with thousands of white topped waves whipped up by the strong wind.. fortunately in my favour... On the right across the lake were more peaks... some with flecks of white on them. The sky was for the most part brilliant blue and I just trotted along gazing at the scene. Then I screeched to a halt... a rainbow... picture time... and I could see where the pot of gold would lie as the rainbow ended in a blur of colours and water spray where the water was blown up by the wind... a little further on was another rainbow ... and as I looked back.. I could see two more. This is the Place where all Rainbows End and it was a silly notion but one that resonated with me and stuck in my head as a really lovely idea.

The road that wound round the Lake was NEVER going to be flat... so it climbed up... wound round and descended again... the wind still at my back... every time I stopped... usually at the top of a rise for a picture.. it hit me hard... as if urging me onward.

One time I stopped for a photo and at least 20 cyclist... unladen... with a support van flashing its hazards.. swept by me. I greeted them as they did me and then started to give chase... the support driver dropped back a little and I managed to find out that they were doing some kind of Christchurch to Christchurch charity ride... at least thats what I think he said. I managed to throw one of my cards into his vehicle and then he sped off. Once again... I tried to chase them down. I wasn't doing too badly but then I thought... ' this scenery is beautiful... this is your last full day cycling...you are never going to keep up with cyclists who have no kit and haven't done 1400ish miles previously.' So I slowed down and then stopped for a photo and enjoyed the spectacular view!

And I kept stopping... because pretty much round every bend was a new view .. even greater than the last. I think .. and maybe I'm biased because of the tailwind.. this was the most beautiful spectacular part of the country that I have seen. There may have been more spectacular bits along the way... just covered in cloud and rain as I went past!!

I drank in the view and it was like regeneration of the soul with every breath... nature coursing through my veins... repairing the broken body from the previous 24 days...

Then the road made a more dramatic climb up... I assume this bit was the Devils Staircase... but actually it wasn't that bad. Whenever I stopped... the wind blew at my back... and the idea got into my head that the strength of the wind helping me up these final hills.. was the strength from everyone back home willing me along. Once again it was perhaps a silly notion but it seems to be the day for those.!

The downward blast was done with a gusting sidewind.. which at the speed I was going caused more than one scary wobble and may me slow down and be slightly more cautious... would be a right bugger to crash now!!

So I tiptoed down... not even worried about the loss of my downhill reward as my reward today was the scenery and the tailwind.

Then I saw two poor buggers.... kitchen sinkers... going the opposite way to me. I shot over and offered sweets etc to mitigate for the fact that they were heading into that wind and probably would be all day. On chatting to them I found out that they were originally from Canada but now lived up Nelson way and were touring the South Island

They had only just set out for the day... so me bouncing over with a grin on my face.. confirming their fears about a headwind all the way down.. probably didn't help!

Kevin and Laureen... nice to meet you briefly.. I sincerely hope the wind dropped or changed direction!!

The cafe at Kingston arrived just in time and I sat down to my usual pancake breakfast and chai. Going to miss that for sure. My thoughts did turn today to the things I will miss about this ride..

The routine of packing up in the morning
The solitude out on the road
Nothing to think of except food miles and sleep
The serene beauty of the road
Blogging every day... putting my thoughts down to clarify them
The rhythm of my legs turning the pedals round
Being exposed to nature...
Breathing the air... watching the sun rise and fall

Then it was back on the road... tailwind still in place and saying goodbye to the Place where Rainbows End ... head forward... metal on the pedals and going for it. I still had a good 70 miles to go. And it was 10:30.

From Kingston the road still wound through the hills... lumpy but with the tailwind unbelievably mainly behind me. As the road twisted and turned it became a sidewind for a bit... Then the valley became wider.. the road now flanked by fields of gold and the hills jutting out beyond them.. some picture postcard moments for sure. Especially now the clouds were beginning to gather .. just to add to the drama. In the far distance I saw lightening but heard no thunder but the sky above was darkening and I felt like I was trying to outrun the storm. It did pour down... but only for 5 minutes and Where was I Hiding?? I was hiding in a cafe in Athol having the most sublime sorbet ice lolly (If anyone finds a source in the UK.. please let me know!!)

After Athol came a succession of small towns until Lumsden at around 14:00 and with 30 miles to go... I felt pretty confident that I'd get there at a reasonable time

Lumsden spoke to me... (yup I have gone road crazy!!) Firstly there was Lydia Street!!!
Then a Route 6 Cafe... complete with American car inside. The sign is following me! Needless to say... I had to eat at the cafe... lunch ... another burger and fries. Im going to have to curb my eating again for sure!!

Then the last 30 miles. At lunch I had booked a room in Winton... partly to ensure some comfort but also partly because my brain was calculating how long it would take to get to Invercargill where Lorraine was staying. Where did you get to? Her question via facebook... well if you look outta your window.....
It would have been funny but possibly not sensible as have some things to do with real world... like checking flights home and making sure I can get home from airport... with my bike!
Incidentally... It did make me laff when Lorraine (staying in Invercargill... waiting to meet me at Bluff)... confessed to dinner of choc liquorice sweets and a bunch of bananas... its not just me that has difficulty finding good road food!

Those 30 miles were mainly flat.. with a couple of longer kick ups ... good for the view at the top... and I blasted them... well until the last 5 ... when my legs gave out and all 1499 ish miles started to tell.

That said I did those thirty miles in under 2 hours 15.. including photo stops!!

I eventually arrived at The Continental Hotel and bar and chatted to the lady in charge. She couldn't give me a discount off the room but the hotel donated $20 to the ride and I got a free evening meal. Thank you!!

Before I ate I wandered along the street to go to Supermarket to pick up a few bits and pieces. I shouldn't be allowed out without my bike and without supervision... I stepped in between 2 kerbs.. scraping all the skin off my left ankle. Typical!!!

So now ensconced in the room... getting prepared for tomorrow (that includes leg shaving(sorry) charging cameras .. phones etc... getting out my spare cycling kit (Lorraine will be pleased that Im not going to sit in her car for 4 hours in my cycling top thats seen me from top to bottom of NZ!) and a myriad of other little things.

So thats the day... for those interested... what follows is a bit about bike and kit! If you really don't care... skip to the last paragraph!

My bike... Giant Defy 1 - 11 speed... 22 gears in all. Possibly could have done with a few more at the lower end but hey... I got up the hills somehow and my knees are intact.

Bags... Apidura done me proud.. pretty waterproof and held up very well. No problems at all. Hardly felt they were there... carried a load of kit. Drew some admiring glances from strangers!!

Bivvy set up... the one time i used it.. brilliant... fast set up and warm and comfortable. Just the sand flies that killed me camping! I would list everything but don't want to really bore everyone... if you are interested in my bivvy set up details.. message me.

TEP portable wifi hotspot... bloody fantastic. Would deffo use again. Well worth the money. Only had trouble one day really.. Haast had no phone signal at all... and slight trouble one other day with slooww connection.

RAVPOWER portable power bank... exceptional ... would definitely use again as holds a huge amount of charge and charges items quickly.

POWERMONKEY solar charger... used a lot in the sunshine on the North Island... really good for rescue charging stuff... i.e not enough charge to power fully but will rescue your phone from 'dead' to 30-40%.

Things I would recommend to take on any long cycle trip like this that I did not take and had to buy...
Bepanthen
High DEET concentration insect repellant

Things I brought but needn't have bothered with .... (some may surprise you)

Spare socks... when off the bike I went sockless...

Underwear for off the bike... like the socks.. I went commando (specifically to allow air to circulate) ... yup even in that posh resort in the North near Taupo !!

Towel... only used once as motels provided towels

Unsure about aero bars... my hands aren't numb .. so maybe they made a small bit of difference... and more practice may prove beneficial.

Ok... WAKE UP!!!!

I can't believe I'm 40 miles from Bluff! This place has been ingrained on my soul. The hard tough days will become the stories told... the people I met... part of the journey... but the beauty and the feel of this country and the emotions it has wrung from me.. will be solely mine... as I cannot explain them to my satisfaction.

Above all ... a lot of money has been raised so far for LHS ... but there is still time to donate
If you can... please go to www.justgiving.com/GoWithTheCrazy
(For anyone reading this now the journey has finished - a donation can be made to Love Hope Strength via Justgiving at https://www.justgiving.com/lhsf *)*

So 40 miles to go....
Today Spiritual regeneration every single time I breathed... New Zealand has imprinted itself on my soul.

LHS xx

This still stands out as one of the best days on my bike ever… the tailwind, the sunshine, the scenery, the nearness of completion combined.

I don't believe that I described 'The Place Where Rainbows End' adequately enough - it defied description and the photos certainly don't do it justice.

I can feel the sadness in my blog as I contemplated returning to 'Life off the road' again but every journey must have an end so that another one can begin.

Day 26
Time to believe

Part 1

There comes a point in any journey like this that you have to believe you will make it to the end....

I hadn't reached that point yet when I woke up this morning. Determined to leave early in case anything should befall me or my bike in the last 40 miles... I went for breakfast at 06:45 only to find that it was too early... so instead I got my last bits and pieces together and head out the door....
20 miles to Invercargill then 20 to Bluff

Keep all fingers and toes crossed..

The words of Mike Peters running round my head as they have every day and through every emotion of this ride...

A tailwind to Invercargill saw me there in just over an hour!! Texted Lorraine... 'Get your arse out of bed... Im at Invercargill'.

Invercargill... quite a nice little town... First traffic lights in a while... must remember to stop... Reading cinemas (my town!) ... disjointed thoughts...

Must take everything in... last day on a bike... some tears... some smiles .. all in remembrance of the days I had felt ...

Last Chai coffee of the trip.... back on the road again... winding road with signs to Bluff! And there in the distance... the end of the road....
See a road going up a huge hill... BEG the cycling gods not to send me up it....

A car driving towards me... the word 'PHOENIX' emblazoned across its bonnet ... I couldn't make it up if I tried...

Headwind!! Just to make sure I truly earn it!

Round the bay... a sign 'BLUFF' ... can it be that I am here??

The song on my Ipod ... The Life you seek does not exist.... what do I seek???

A climb... of course... on smooooooth town tarmac... and up round the corner and over the top and there were the signposts and standing nearby... waving at me ....Lorraine....

Stop... legs stopped... no more pedal turns to take.... I kept on Cycling To The End!!

Just some of the thoughts that rattled through my head... written like they occurred to me. Seeing Lorraine there to meet me was like having someone I'd known for years to welcome me in and just so happy to see her... Thank you Lorraine

Then the inevitable pictures and minutes to take it in... to store up for later when my brain could process it all better..

Lorraine then said 'Right lets see if the bike fits in the car!!' So funny!! It did fit and I was soon ensconced in a nice warm comfy car... rattling along at speeds I could only generate downhill ... peddling for all I was worth and with a rocket booster on the back!

After a while my arse hurt!! I couldn't easily perform the two cheek shuffle either... a blanket was dug out to provide some padding... which greatly helped the issue.
We chatted for the three or so hours it took to drive to Andy and Julie's House. Andy and Auden guitars organised the gig tonight but more about that later... for the story now... they had kindly allowed basically a stranger to pitch up at their house... shower... change

191

.. drink coffee and then bugger off to the gig!

Greeted initially by Andy's mum and then Julie when she got back... I was made to feel at home and welcome. I felt a bit at 6's and 7's... not quite sure what to do with myself. Having showered and changed into the gig clothes I had sent to Andy's house... I felt weird without my LHS cycle jersey ... so decided to wear that (the clean one) and my gloves to the gig..

Then myself and Lorraine went for a quick tourist stop..... the Steepest Street in the world... average 35% gradient with a section of 38% ... I would like to claim that it was a shame I didn't have my bike!!!!

Then onto Coronation Hall and the gig....

Part 2

Before I blog about the gig.. there is a huge long list of people I need to thank... so please bear with me.... In no particular order....

Mum,Dad, Paul (bro), Jax, Danny boy, Nath, Banna girl and Nathan.... better family I could not choose. X

My work mothers (Denise and Jilly) and Solder... I am so lucky to have you guys propping me up.. X

Dave Spragg... My inspiration. X

Mike and Jules Peters... for the music and LHS! You have both inspired me to really live life. Mike your music and words have weaved through this journey and once again given me strength. Just so lucky to be a part of it all. Thankyou X

Mickey .. for the bug higs x

David and Nicola... for support... messages and always going with the crazy... Its alright... Its ok! X

Mark and Sue Hobbs.. for picking me up... welcoming me into this country and becoming instant friends and going above and beyond to help me. X

Roger... for being a kind New Zealander and checking I was ok on the road! X

Mary and Alec... for coming across country to meet a crazy stranger and being that piece of home. X

To everyone who has.. donated... liked... shared... talked about and given words of encouragement... This journey is also yours as I couldn't have done it without you. X

Doug from Auden... for making it possible. X

Lorraine... for being the person to welcome me at the end... for the stories and laughter we shared x

Andy and Julie... for the gig.. but more importantly for the friendship offered and the comfort given when it all became too much... that meant so very much to me. X

Part 3

So its 2am and I sit here blogging... trying to put my thoughts down on paper but words may fail me...

It was somewhat a daze... dreamworld... adrenaline high...a mixture of all the above that I landed in Coronation Hall to be greeted by a lovely gentleman wearing one of my promo t shirts! Andy from Auden Guitars had been sorting out this evening from the very early days of ride planning and I greatly appreciate his efforts.

3 bands had kindly donated their time this evening... Valley Bluegrass... Melissa Partridge and The Eastern with maybe a surprise thrown in the mix... if I had the balls!

Valley Bluegrass kicked the evening off and the lively tunes got the feet tapping...

Melissa was up next... What a beautiful voice... and some lovely songs of country rock type stuff. Thank you for supporting LHS X

I was a bundle of nerves... determined to sing and attempt to play (with shaking.. slightly numb fingers (thats my excuse anyway) a song that I wrote. The hands were shaking so badly... it all went wrong from a playing point of view at times... okay most the song.. but encouraged by an understanding audience ... I hope I did my Phoenix proud. The video has been posted unreviewed/unedited on my facebook page... www.facebook.com/OneChallengeAtATime

It came from the heart and is what it is.

Then the Eastern... what energy!

And then a song and some words that prompted the tears to flow...

And it all suddenly overwhelmed me and I sat there... head in hands... surrounded by a room full of strangers but at the same time amongst friends. I cant describe the emotions but they were whirling through head.. heart ... soul. All that I am... all I will ever be ... are words that come to mind. And two friends flanking me... silent comfort... thank you

And then a song and words that prompted a smile....

And I was sitting there with the thought of how the world can have great beauty in such simple things...

A shared cause... a shared love of music...

This ride and the people I have met along the way and the support from back home have once again renewed... rebuilt... my faith in humanity and the good that can be created.

If just one person from the gig takes on board the message of Love Hope and Strength and shares it around... or one person signs up to GET ON THE LIST...or ... or... then who knows what it may lead to...

LOVE HOPE STRENGTH

Three words... put together... Save Lives .. and provide an inspiration and foundation. Check it out... www.lovehopestrength.co.uk

It's now 02:40 and I'm still awake and buzzin!

Tomorrow I will add thoughts once things have settled.

For now...

Fight the fear... Embrace the Randomness and above all
Go With The Crazy!

Day 27
There's still so much more to be said...

... all the lines are in my head.....

But organising them and getting them onto 'paper' is difficult... yet I cannot give up the blogging just yet... I am not yet right back where I started from...

Perhaps this is the beginning of yet another chapter in the book of my life but I'm not quite ready to turn the page from the last and desperately cling to parts of it... my arms tightly around as long as possible.

I received message from a very good friend this morning which not only tipped me over the edge into tears again ... blaming lack of sleep this time... but part of what he said I wish to share with you (I hope he doesn't mind) as it struck me...

He said that they were on the outside looking into my journey and that they only got to see and feel a small part of the journey... like watching the film version of a book where you don't really get the story the author wrote.

And part of me wished I could explain bits better or hadn't been so tired at the end of the day... or had such a crap memory that I forgot some of it (like the kiwi sense of humour that called two tumbling waterfalls at the side of the road... 'trickle 1' and 'trickle 2'!)

But then part of me thought that if it left some interpretation they could attach their own meaning to my vague ramblings and maybe gain more out of it.. than just my vague ramblings - like modern art?? Lol

And so I find myself sitting in Brisbane Airport (I bought a fridge magnet cos this counts as having been to Australia!) with so much more to be said and all the lines in my head but maybe not converting into a full set of lyrics.

This morning was very strange... I had only really got to sleep at 0300 and woke pretty much every hour until I gave up about half six and started organising stuff into packing piles.. stuff to go in with bike... stuff for my seat bag... and stuff for my rucksack... Andy (from Auden guitars) and Julie had been kind enough to let me crash overnight and were taking me to the Airport in the afternoon.. to begin my long journey home.

It was strange not to have anywhere to get to... strange not to have to worry about headwinds... hills... and a sore arse. In fact I already felt a loss... of freedom... and air to breathe... and beautiful scenery. The pain and effort already half forgotten. Im not sure I can describe adequately how free and alive it can make you feel... to push yourself and challenge yourself... to the point of breaking... standing on the edge and inching that little bit further..

I also cant thank Andy and Julie enough for having me to stay and sharing the end of the journey with me... There are many others I wish could have been there too. But with Lorraine.. Andy and Julie .. I was amongst friends.

We had breakfast...(must get out of that habit again) and then went for a little walk before dropping another friend of theirs off at the airport (his flight a few hours before mine). The walk was to the top of a hill where the views stretched out for an almost 360 degree panorama. It was sunny and cloudless and a perfect way to end my trip.
It felt like New Zealand was saying goodbye and come back sometime!

We dropped Chris off at the airport... which I will describe in a bit... and then went for a quick stroll round this beautiful lake... busy with at least 50 people there... I was being reintroduced to a non solo cycling lifestyle bit by bit. After that we went had lunch at a pub sooo busy (think Reading pub on a Monday lunchtime) that we were asked to get our orders in as quick as possible!

We then went to check me and my bike in!

I like being early so it was with some consternation that Andy and Julie suggested we go back to their house for coffee after checking the bike in and watching it be carted away. (In addition Julie had written the words on it.. ' This bike has taken Lydia from North to South New Zealand for Love Hope Strength... ' it almost made me cry... again... once again on a knife edge of surging emotions.

The coffee turned out to be a great idea as I got to pick up a table tennis bat ... having had a gauntlet thrown down at my feet by their son. It was with some satisfaction that I managed to draw one game all... no time for a third game... and my ego intact! Thanks bud.. it was fun!

Then back to the airport ... where cows bordered the runway ... there was one gate for international flights and parking was actually at the airport... not miles away. A far cry from Heathrow and therefore very nice and peaceful... no scrum at security either.
Before that I had to say goodbye to Andy and Julie and given that we had really only just met... it seemed that I was saying cheerio to lifelong friends (probably just me... they most likely opened a good bottle of wine to celebrate!) Julie bought me a bracelet of hematite stones... a silvery/grey/black colour and very pretty.. thank you very much.
And then I was once again a solo traveller...

The flight to Brisbane was short... at least by my standards over the next day.. 4 hours. Probably long enough for the nice gentleman sat next to me in my unwashed off bike clothes to regret it..

And so I sit freezing in the airport... still contemplating. It took all of the four hour flight to come up with a title for the blog today and the important thing to impart from this journey... the main line still in my head...

Life is short... seize every moment... love .. live.. laugh...dream aloud... see life in colour... and do all of those things with your whole heart and soul because if you do not throw all of yourself in.... you risk nothing and gain little. Make Love Hope and Strength part of your daily life ... impart it to others and gain it in return... Fight the fear.. Embrace the Randomness and Go With The Crazy!

Mike Peters and Love Hope Strength Foundation give people a chance to fight back against cancer by swabbing people for the bone marrow donor list and raising money and awareness across the globe. Mike inspires many of us to follow his example and we have embraced LHS as part of us and along the way found many lifelong friends.

We are always looking for volunteers to help us... people to join us at our Rocks Events and to help us spread the word of LHS. To find out more about the charity please go to www.lovehopestrength.co.uk or www.lovehopestrength.org for the USA site.

If you have enjoyed my ramblings over the past weeks and feel able to donate... www.justgiving.com/GoWithTheCrazy. (*For anyone reading this now the journey has finished - a donation can be made to Love Hope Strength via Justgiving at* https://www.justgiving.com/lhsf *)*

One Challenge At A Time will continue to Dream Aloud and plans are already being hatched ... This is the game I choose to play!

"You've got to take life and ride it till the wheels fall off"

BRAD SIMMS

Save All your Crying For Later

It has been around a week since my bike ride ended and I landed at Heathrow to the news that I'd lost my best friend to Cancer.

Needless to say the news had a huge impact on me and adjusting back into a post bike ride world - which can be a strange adjustment at the best of times... but more about that in a bit.

He would hate for me to say anything but as I am me, I must say a few words and he would understand.

Those of you that knew him would agree that he was one of the kindest men that lived and a shining example of how to deal with the shit that life throws at you with a smile. Keep smiling was our watchword and he lived by it.

For me - he was my inspiration on how to live life - even when hit by the impact that a cancer diagnosis can have. He gave me strength and courage to continue on my tough days both from his words and his example, and a smile to help. My world will be a much poorer/greyer place without him but I will carry my memories of him and the time I was so lucky to spend with him, with me in every CraZy endeavour in the future whilst aiming to make him proud. I am so glad that he got to see that I had finished the ride. It was for him.

And so ....
The bike ride itself was one of the toughest things I have ever done. the weather (rain and scorching heat), illness, bad drivers (1 accident), bees and more 'hills' than I have ever encountered on a bike.

The final stats according to my Garmin for those of you that are interested were:

Total mileage: 1575.9
Average moving speed: 11.9 mph
Max speed: 67.3 mph (how and where I don't know)

Other stats include:

Times chased by dogs: 1
Knocked off bike: 1
Bee Stings:1
Punctures: 0 (unbelievably)
Injuries: 0
Tubes of Chammy cream used: 2.5
Mosquito/sandfly bites: must have numbered over 100
Moments where I truly wanted to give up: 2

Best moment: Getting to the top of the Rimutaka 'Hill'
Worst moment: Haast Pass (wet/cold/tired and pushing my bike)

Bottles of Fcuk It Juice used - At least 2

Daily calorie consumption Estimate:8000-10000

money raised: Over £2500 and counting

The ride ebbed and flowed to the music and lyrics of Mike Peters - my other inspiration. Another man who sees the positive in everything, an experience to be had in everything and lives life to the full, whilst inspiring everyone around him to follow his example. i couldn't have done the ride without the inspiration, comfort and strength his lyrics provided on a daily basis and I feel privileged to be a small part of the whirlwind surrounding LHS and The Alarm.

The support from family and friends, both back home and people I had met along the way was once again the highlight and made this endeavour, turning the pedals until the end, one which affirmed my faith in the basic goodness of people and the world. Again, I could not have completed the ride without this support.

Adjusting back into the world of work, household chores etc is not an easy one anyway. Gone is the routine of the road, the rhythm of turning the pedals, the vast space around you, the peace of being alone in nature and with just the road, the music and my thoughts for company. Once back, life explodes from the basics of finding food and shelter and worries about the weather and mileage into the complicated crazy mess that life is. The memories of the pain and suffering in the ride fade in, fade out and fade away, leaving only the memories of the sun shining down, a kind word or a smile along the way, the feeling of my phoenix hovering above keeping an eye on me or the view that took my breath away. These are the moments in time that I live for and cherish. This time, the person that I would have shared all this with has gone, leaving me feeling bereft and needing to find an inner Strength that surpasses anything I needed to find on my ride.

Part of that strength comes from continuing to volunteer with LHS, knowing that it was a cause close to his heart as well. With the tour Alarm/Stranglers now up and running I will have something to focus on and pour my energy into. That and the planning of my next crazy adventure, which will be longer, harder and once again - push me to the absolute limits. If your dreams don't scare you, they aren't big enough!

As I said in my previous blogs... and what has been hammered home ... is that LIFE IS SHORT! Cram as much in as possible, experience everything and Fight the Fear, love with all your heart, live with every fibre of your being, cherish friends, family and loved ones because this wonderful world can be so unkind.

This will be the last of my New Zealand blogs but It's alright.. It's ok... there will be more Crazy adventures and stories to tell, so keep an eye on my facebook page, for updates on the CraZy.
www.facebook.com/OneChallengeAtATime

Planning is already underway - this is the way of life.

If you haven't yet donated, there is still time - www.justgiving.com/GoWithTheCrazy - we can Fight back with Love Hope and Strength together. I hope you have enjoyed this journey along with me. (*For anyone reading this now the journey has finished - a donation can be made to Love Hope Strength via Justgiving at* https://www.justgiving.com/lhsf)

And that is where the blogs of this journey end....

3 months later and it seems like a lifetime ago that I raised my leg over my bike to begin this journey. Writing this book has been at times an emotional experience, raising memories up from the recesses of my mind where I have hidden them but it has also been a cathartic one - reminding me of the beauty in humankind and of this world that we inhabit. Some of the memories are so vivid, I can feel the rain or hear the wind whistling in my ears, drowning out all thought... some pictures of the road jump back into my head in a stark reminder.. some memories have faded.

Did I learn anything about myself? Yes I did, but nothing I could necessarily articulate successfully. My inner strength has been fortified by the experience and hardened me again to pain and suffering.

I miss the road... but I have not been idle. As one journey ends, another inevitably begins and Dreams are being put into the planning phase.

The Tour Divide is starting to consume my waking and sleeping thoughts and training has begun. The transformation of dream to actuality has begun and is relentless. As mentioned, this is a race, described as 'The toughest Bike Race in The World' and with good reason. 40% of participants do not make it to the finish line - will I be one of that 40% next year?

Life begins at the end of your comfort zone and I get the feeling that I have possibly been kidding myself before... this one is so far out of my comfort zone that it stretches into the stratosphere....

My new bike... a mountain bike, hardtail 29er. I have already added a dynamo hub and USB charger onto it with the Tour divide at the forefront of my thoughts. Training in the art of mountain biking has begun with many days spent out riding the trails of varying difficulty and with varying success. One big crash so far resulted in only bruises and dented pride and for certain it won't be the last as I try to become the master of my new mode of transport.

Mountain biking required an all over body fitness - this time it's not just about the legs and although I have been practicing tricky single track, the Tour Divide is mainly on gravel roads and fire roads with some single track thrown in... and oh the climbing...Equivalent of climbing Everest from sea-level 7 times, this is a ride of EPIC proportions that one may be described as CraZy to even think about lining up at the start.
But that is what I intend to do....

The 2700 mile route takes in some of the wildest and remote countryside on the planet. The record time for a woman is 15 days and 17 hours (or something like that) and a respectable time is considered to be up to double of the record time. I will be aiming for 20 days - an ambitious aim, but I might as well go for extra-crazy!

I continue to write blogs and updates - all of which can be found on my Facebook page - www.facebook.com/OneChallengeAtATime and I hope that you will join with me in the route to another great journey.

Before I put my final words down on paper to close this chapter - I must thank several people above and beyond the thanks I extend to everyone who supported me on this ride and in life (you know who you are I hope)

Firstly a massive thank you to David and Nicola Johnston who have joined in with some of the Crazy, inspired some of the CraZy and helped me through some tough times.

Another massive thank you goes to Nicky Pritchard for providing the excellent artwork for the cover of the book, capturing the essence of the ride perfectly.

Finally the third massive thank you goes to Mickey Collins, known to have done some CraZy stuff in the name of charity (mankini and bike ring any bells?). Mickey proof read a draft of this book and provided some fantastic critique (as he did for my previous book) but more importantly chose an inspired title, when my inspiration had dried up.

All we have is Time - words sung by the inspirational Mike Peters…. it's our job to make the best of what time we have - you never know when it will be gone.

Heartfelt thanks again to everyone for sharing and being part of this journey with me - I could not have done it without your support and encouragement.

There is only one way to bring this journey to a close and that is to leave the final words to the man whose music and lyrics once again weaved their way through this ride as they do my life….

Stay Free… Stay Alive

Lightning Source UK Ltd.
Milton Keynes UK
UKOW05f0848251016

286086UK00012B/170/P